Road Rage
Las Vegas:
The Senseless
Murder of Tammy Meyers

BOOK ONE

MARK FIERRO

Author: Mark Fierro
Editor: Jeff Haney
Cover design: Michael D. Durant

ISBN: 1517459095
ISBN-13: 978-1517459093

DEDICATION

Dedicated to the memory
of Tammy Meyers.

"I really wish you could have met her."

— Kristal Meyers, daughter

CONTENTS

"Monsters come in all shapes and sizes. Sometimes monsters are things people should be scared of, but they aren't."

Neil Gaiman,
The Ocean at the End of the Lane

CHAPTER 1
THE ROAD

Bob Meyers and his son Robert were working in Kernville, California, a small town in the Southern Sierra Nevada Mountains, on the night of February 12, 2015. It had been an unusually warm day in the scenic riverside town and the warmth had hung on as midnight approached. The two had spent hours setting up the family's booth for their business, for which they traveled from town to town for conventions and community events, selling sports memorabilia and related items. It was a rare night when Bob wouldn't have his wife Tammy at his side, especially when they had business out on the road, but she had to stay behind in Las Vegas this time to take one of their children to the dentist.

As Bob is quick to admit, Tammy was the executive of the operation, a natural born salesperson, marketer, inventory control expert and dealmaker. Gregarious and quick to smile, Tammy was a dynamo of energy who was always on the lookout to help people. Anybody, anytime. Bob kept to the driving and the heavy lifting. Between them, their close circle of friends literally ran to the hundreds.

Bob and Robert were putting the finishing touches on their display for the next day. In the next minute, their lives would change forever. Bob got a phone call from his 15-year-old daughter Kristal. She was hysterical, and to add to the pressure, the cell phone coverage was spotty. Before the phone died, Bob managed to make out only bits and pieces: "Some guy" ran into them with his car or threatened to kill them. The pressure in Bob's chest ratcheted up a few notches when Bob called Tammy's cell. His wife's phone was dead.

Seconds later, their son Matthew was on the line. Matthew blurted out, "Dad, mom's been shot." That Bob heard loud and clear. Matthew couldn't go into details because he was at the house where other family members, including Bob's elderly mother, were within range. Bob Meyers recalled, "He said it was bad. At that time, I'm freaking out. OK, was she shot in the arm? The leg?" Matthew didn't know. The one thing that stuck: "It was bad."

Upon hearing the call, Bob's son Robert was panic-stricken. Both men were dumbstruck as they started tearing through preparations to leave. They had made the drive out from Las Vegas to Kernville in a leisurely six-and-a-half hours through the desert highlands and California hills and mountain passes. They would make the trip back to Las Vegas in under five hours.

"I left all the trailer doors open, everything," Bob recalled. "I called a friend who was up there setting up, and he went over and secured the trailer. I just left everything behind.

"I'm pretty much hysterical. People were trying to call me, I'm trying to call them, a Las Vegas Metropolitan Police officer tried to call me but the call almost immediately dropped because we're up in the mountains. I was driving about 100 mph up through those mountain passes. There were about 45 minutes when we couldn't connect with anybody. All we knew was that their mom was in deep trouble. I kept hearing the replay over and over and over: 'It's bad.' "

The pressure was every bit as bad for Robert, who could hear every word of the urgent, emotional phone calls on the truck's hands-free system. But all the calls seemed to drop just at the critical juncture. What Bob wasn't sharing with his son on the breakneck drive through the mountains was one nagging fact: Tammy rarely went anywhere without at least one of the kids.

Were the kids OK? What wasn't being said?

Bob recalled, "I just wanted to know what the hell was going on but I was scared to death every time the phone rang."

Finally, the two cleared the worst of the mountains and almost immediately the phone rang with a call from police.

"The Las Vegas officer was standing next to Matthew, but he wouldn't give me any information," Bob said. "He said detectives would call me. Then I hit a stretch that put us back in the mountains again, it seemed like forever, maybe another hour, where I couldn't get any reception.

"It was hell. The next call I had was from a reporter who was standing next to Matthew a hundred yards from the house.

"What came out of the reporter's mouth was, 'What are your feelings on your wife being shot in the head?' This is while I'm driving, trying to get home. 'Shot in the head.' "

The human mind has amazing defense mechanisms. Bob kept hearing Matthew's voice: "It's bad." Maybe it was going to mean a long recovery. Maybe it was that kind of bad. They could live with that. No one said Tammy was dying, so there was that much to hang onto.

"Despite the calls I didn't want to know," Bob said. "But I knew. I kept pushing it back. 'It's bad.' 'Your wife has been shot in the head.' I was clinging to hope. I mean, I'm hanging on with everything I have. I'm lying to myself. I found out through Matthew and a reporter that Tammy was taken to the hospital. I called University Medical Center but it took me 15 minutes to get through to the right person because of the security protocols they put in place when someone is shot and the suspect isn't in custody. They had Tammy come in as a Jane Doe for her protection. Her attackers were still out there, loose."

Bob Meyers was looking for a break, some ray of hope, at least a glimmer, that would never come. Bit by bit, call by call, the last few shreds of hope were being worn away with each static-filled cell call. He finally found someone with direct knowledge of Tammy's medical condition, and it hit as hard as anything he had heard from that night into the early morning hours.

"The UMC nurse was very businesslike, very clinical. As bad as the news was, I appreciated her honesty. She said, 'Your wife has been involved in a shooting. She's been shot in the head. It's serious.' They asked me where I was at. They told me to pull over and at that second I knew. I knew."

There were no more mental hiding places.

"I said I didn't have time to pull over, just tell me. That's when they told me it doesn't look good. And that's when I started breaking down a little bit.

"I told the nurse, 'I don't care what you guys have to do, keep her going until I get there. Do what you have to do.' They told me the doctors were in there with her, they couldn't talk to me. And it was quite serious. And that I needed to get there when I could get there."

It says something about your life when you don't have the luxury of having a breakdown. Responsibilities to his kids and specifically 21-year-old Robert, who was learning everything about his mother's critical condition as quickly as his father, loomed large on Bob's mind.

"They are going to learn through my reaction to this," Bob said. "They are watching every move and I have to be as strong as ever for them. Rhino skin.

"Next a police officer called me, asked me where I was at, and I told him. He explained that, as they understood it, there was a road rage incident of some sort and that my wife was shot in front of our house.

I said, 'How was it a road rage if she was shot in front of my house?' He said, 'You'll have to ask the detectives that.' I said I needed to talk to my son and my daughter. He said, 'You can't at this time. Detectives aren't going to let you do that.' I said that my daughter is 15, she's a minor, and I don't want people talking to her unless I'm there."

Kristal was always considered the baby of the family. Until this night she had lived a protected life, shielded by three big brothers who were taught from the day Kristal was born to "always stick up for your little sister." In the days to come, Kristal would be the focus of some of the worst of the taunting and adolescent insults on social media.

At this time, with about three hours remaining in a five-hour drive, Bob learned how bad it was for his wife of nearly 25 years.

"That's when the police officer told me Tammy wasn't going to make it. I had it on Bluetooth. And I'm driving so fast, there's no time to hold the phone. So my son Robert is hearing all this as it happens.

"We were going through the Tehachapi Mountains at that time, outside Bakersfield. I'm driving the truck, Robert is sitting to my right. He's hysterical and there's not a damn thing in the world I can do for my boy."

In the weeks and months to come, Bob Meyers would reflect that there was no easy way to tell someone that a loved one wasn't going to live, but of all the ways he could imagine, he felt his son Robert had learned in the worst way possible.

The defense mechanisms came flooding back in. "What was going through my mind at that time was just how strong my wife is and that she'll pull through it. I know her. I'm hoping the whole time it's not that bad. I'm lying to myself to get through the next mile. The truth is, I'm just hoping I don't get that phone call saying she passed before we could get there. At that moment, there is nothing in the world I fear more than that phone ringing again."

It's come down to this: At this point, the truth is that the father and son were simply hoping to get to say a last goodbye.

"I don't know any of the details," Bob said. "I don't know who saw what. I wasn't getting any answers. I tried to reach the officer who called me, but there was no answer. For a little while there, there was nothing.

"All I knew was that the kids were always with her. So Brandon could have been hurt. Would they keep that from us? I was hoping against hope. It just gets worse and worse as time goes on.

"Finally I had a clear shot. Someone who would give me everything I had to know. I had a friend get down to the hospital. He got a hold of me, and I was on the I-15 at the time, near Barstow. He told me to pull over, and again I said no. He said drive safe, when you get here, you get here, but it's pretty bad.

"I asked him, 'Is she gonna make it?' My friend is a straightforward kind of man. He said, 'I don't think so, Bob.' He got down there pretty quick, him and his wife, and saw everything. It was pretty graphic. Be very careful what you wish for. I wanted to know. Now I knew.

"One of the violent crimes detectives called me, said there was an investigation. Explained what happened. They said it wasn't a homicide yet because she was still alive. I said, 'You have my number, call me. I'm driving right now.' And they hadn't explained how my wife was shot in front of the house, out front. They just said the house, exiting the car.

"They asked me if there was any reason anyone would want to harm my wife. I said, 'Are you freaking kidding me?' "

There was, finally, one break for Bob Meyers that night. The police officer could give him an accurate accounting of his children and his 75-year-old mother.

"He did tell me my mom was OK, Brandon was OK, Kristal was OK. They were being taken by patrol car to the hospital to be with their mother. I had spoken to Matthew, and Robert is right by my side, so I knew everybody except Tammy was OK. We had that, and that was a very real, a huge concern.

"My son Matthew called back. He was upset because they wouldn't allow him to go to the house, so he was heading to the hospital. When he called from the hospital, he was panic-stricken, he was so upset I couldn't even understand what he was saying. When I think back to that night I really feel horrible for Matthew. He was completely alone. His mother was dying. He, more than anyone, was in a position to know that. None of us could be there for him. It was his 20th birthday."

Bob Meyers and his four kids knew enough to know they didn't want to know any more. It could only get worse.

"Every time the phone rings, we're going through the roof. We're just waiting for that bad call, you know. We have to be able to say goodbye. God, at least give me that."

With his wife clinging to life by a thread and those first few hours of pushing his luck through the hairpin turns of the mountain ranges of the Sequoia National Forest and the Tehachapis, something had to give. It came way down the road on the Baker grade. It was on the long climb to the summit on the I-15 that one of the two turbos on the Meyers' big Ford truck blew up. Uhhhhhhhhhhhh.

"I'll be honest, I'm going 100 mph plus. And when I hit the I-15, I redlined it all the way from Barstow on past Baker so that's like 60 miles plus. I was pushing it so hard and driving so fast I blew the turbo. It just got too hot."

Bob and Robert, with the crushing wait of an additional hour added to their arrival at the hospital, would have to limp along at a maddeningly slow pace.

Just as the pair hit the state line at Primm the phone rang and both men jumped through the roof.

"It was a call from Kristal using my friend's phone. She was far more collected, which somehow seemed to make the situation far more desperate. She said, 'Daddy you need to get here. Mommy is in bad, bad shape. She's bleeding very bad.' Kristal's 15 at this point. I would have given anything in the world to spare her this."

Finally the Ford limped in to University Medical Center, the region's top-rated trauma center. Doctors here routinely see in a week what some trauma centers see in a year. Car wreck, gunshot, the litter of good times gone bad in Las Vegas.

"We pull in and I just parked where the ambulances park. There were probably 50 friends there and about 20 reporters with cameras and blinding camera lights. I didn't know what to expect but I sure as hell didn't expect to see that. The reporters didn't know who I was until my friends came up on me and were trying to console us. That's when the media descended and everything went crazy like in the movies. My friends shielded me and we just marched inside. It was on. They were shouting questions at me. The only thing I could think was, 'Don't they realize my wife is dying?' That second voice says, 'Bob, your wife is dying and that's the only reason they are here.'

"That's my introduction to the media. They have their job. I get that. What they don't know is that they might as well have been throwing ball-peen hammers at my head. None of this crap is important to me. I just wanted to get inside to see my wife. Once inside the door, a detective came up to me like he's going to play middle linebacker. He says, 'We need to talk.' I'm like, 'Hell yeah, we need to talk, I'm going to talk your hair off, but right now, I'm going to see my wife before she dies.'

"I made it this far and after 25 years of marriage she isn't going to die without us seeing each other one more time. I want to make something clear here, I love the police. Not some, but a lot of my friends are police and retired police. My people. But this guy is standing between me and my wife of 25 years and, based on what I have heard at this point, she could take her last breath at any second."

Whatever else University Medical Center is, it's also pretty secure. If officials don't want Bob coming in, Bob isn't coming in.

"Because the detective is talking to me, the security of the hospital wouldn't open the doors, so I look over at the security guy. I said, 'You have 3 seconds to open the door.' He looked over at the detective. I said, 'You're down to 2 seconds now.' Then I went up to the door, and the detective must have waved him off because I just pried it open and walked in.

"Tammy was behind a secure door in the Intensive Care Unit. It was a private room. It's a pretty intense place. It's where the worst of the worst cases, life-threatening injuries go. It's brighter than the noonday sun. It's so bright it's like being inside of a light bulb. Bright white. Kristal comes running up to me and then friends and family.

"They had a couple Metro guys camped outside her room and about three hospital security guards plus the two guards who escorted me to the room. This just can't be real. This is from a movie, this isn't us. This isn't me and Tammy and the kids. Our lives are filled with friends, laughing, kids, our kids' friends, our friends' kids *are* our kids. This isn't us. This is some kind of setup for people who do terrible things who are involved in crime. That night I came to learn that a lot of completely innocent people come here to die for no good reason whatsoever.

"Then I get to the room where my Tammy is. It's us. It's real. Now, it's real. Christ.

"She was surrounded by friends, about 20 people who they allowed in there. I was really happy for that. I couldn't take it if she was alone or just with people she didn't know. These are the people we love all pulling for Tammy. No media was allowed inside. The only ones inside the actual room were Brandon, Kristal, my mom and mother-in-law. Three nurses.

"This is it. I walk in. God my wife is dying. Tammy was hooked up to a lot of machines. This big bandage around her whole head and the side of her face. With blood on the bandage. She is out. Not moving. But I could tell she was still in there alive. I swear with all I have, I know she was still in there. It wasn't just a feeling. It was knowing.

"I didn't lose it right there because my kids were there. When I walked in the room I said, 'I'm here, baby.' She started shaking, you know. Then I held her hand. She kept shaking it. I told her, I said, 'You know I'm here. Baby, I'm here.' She had no movement before that. None. No movement of any kind until I got there. I asked the nurse. Before this second, she was not moving. The nurse was telling me, 'She knows you're here. She knows.' Jesus, what are we going to do?

"The nurses approached me and said the doctor needed to talk to me right now. The doctors said, 'Do you know what Tammy's record is as a potential organ donor?' I said, 'Whoa, whoa, back up here. Tell me what's going on.'

"They said she had been shot in the side of her head. It went through her temple. It turns out that the .45-caliber bullet that she had been shot with had shattered her nose and took out her right eye and her ear. All I can hear is the voice in my head saying, 'For what? For what?'

"I hear myself say, 'Well what do we do?' They said, right now as it sits, the prognosis is that Tammy is not going to recover. I said, 'Well, she's been here for this period of time, I want a second team of doctors in.' And the doctor told me, 'Well this is it, we have three teams in here.' I said, 'I'll get on the phone to another hospital. Get another doctor.' That's what I had my friend do, get a second opinion. Don't give up, don't give up, don't give up. It's all I can think of for Tammy and for my kids and me.

"That's when I walked out of that room and I broke down. I walked out of the whole emergency area. I walked outside, blind to the world just to be alone and

I walked … right into the cameras. Just what I needed. Everybody is screaming at me. Me and my family are the soup of the day. This is where the security at the hospital was so great. The guard knew I was lost, he grabbed me and pulled me back, put me in a little room they had. I went in there. I was alone. I broke down. I lost it. This is it. There is nothing, nothing left.

"I guess I am as lost as I have ever been. I know there's all this technology and everything, and I know how strong my wife is. I don't want these people to give up. I was upset mostly with myself because I wasn't there to protect my wife and my family. If you have never lost someone close, really close, let me tell you, you always think it's all your fault. If I had just … Every one of my kids has it. It's the exercise we do now instead of sleeping.

"That's when I started asking questions. I wanted to know what happened. Brandon and Kristal were both breaking down. I couldn't get the whole story. I was getting bits and pieces. I asked one of the Metro officers and he says I need to ask the detective. I called back the detective and asked him what he had so far. He says, 'Your wife and daughter were involved in a road rage incident.' They didn't disclose that Brandon had gone out with Tammy after. Just that my daughter and wife were involved in a road rage case, and the guy had followed them home and shot my wife.

"I got with my friends and said, 'We've got to figure this out now. Something is not adding up, you know?' It just didn't make sense.

"I remember the phone call I had got from Kristal earlier, and she was at home. And I'm like … something isn't flying here. That's when I started sending my friends out to find out what happened.

"By now it's daylight, 6 or 7 in the morning. I hadn't left the hospital at all. The media is still out there. I'm holed up there. I sent the kids and my mom and mother-in-law home with some friends.

"This is the one thing I knew for certain from talking to the police: These guys who shot my wife in the head are still out there. So I told my friends, 'I have to stay with Tammy. You guys watch my family.'

"It was a few days after before I slept. I came home to check on the kids a couple times. I stayed there pretty much 24 hours, sitting at her side at the hospital. A few friends inside with us, Metro outside the door. There was nothing but us and medical equipment. No television so I had no idea what was going on in the case from the media perspective. There was always two nurses in the room, too. The door was wide open and another nurse was sitting right outside with the machine. She had a minimum of three nurses at all times. These are really good, really caring professionals. These nurses are really something. As a former nurse, Tammy would have given the thumbs up.

"When I did go home, I stayed home for about five hours. I got a call from the other doctor my friends and I had arranged for and I met him down there at the hospital. When I got down there he said that

Tammy's brain was pushed toward the rear of her skull. Really bad. And he told me straight up, 'There's nothing we can do to bring her back. Nothing we can do.'

"I know what I'm about to tell you may sound like wishful thinking. Tammy is lying there with horrible wounds but I don't care what anybody thinks. I know what was going on between us. Tammy was trying to tell me something, you know? She kept shaking in my hand. Nothing had moved since she arrived. Nothing but her hand that was in mine was moving. I was talking to her, but not about what happened. I was telling her how much I loved her and how happy I was that we had a life together. But I know she was trying to say something to me. She couldn't get anything out, not in words, but we had a long conversation. With the hand squeezes, I know she was trying to tell me what happened. To tell me she loved me, things will be OK, because that's the kind of person she was. We said plenty. If you've been with somebody your whole life, you know exactly what I'm talking about."

CHAPTER 2
BETTER DAYS

Bob Meyers recalls that he caught his first real break in life as a 24-year-old standing 6-foot-4, driving a truck and playing basketball as a full-contact sport in the City of Industry in Southern California. For such a young man he was pretty focused. He never drank much, and he had managed to hold down a condo in Azusa, a pleasant foothill suburb at the northeast corner of the Los Angeles County line. That's when he first saw a neighbor. It seemed to Bob she kept kind of popping up.

"I was all about work, work, work. I've always been that way. I worked six days a week then. Work and playing basketball. If I wasn't working I was playing basketball. If I wasn't playing basketball I was working. I had a group of friends in my city and we'd play other guys from other cities. We called ourselves the Sparks. I played center. I'm 6-4, and weighed about 235 then. I was pretty aggressive on the court, the big guy. I guess you could say that I was one of those guys who didn't take a whole lot of shit."

Meyers was always looking for a way up, a way to advance his career and potential. He got into bounty hunting for a bit, where his size and athleticism gave him a leg up on the streets. He worked some security gigs from time to time but mostly had his eyes open for opportunity. He was never afraid of hard work.

In 1990 Bob was making the rounds: "I was just dating a couple of women casually, nothing special.

One day when we had just wrapped up a game, one of my friends from the team who also worked with me sees Tammy at my complex as she goes walking past my door. He had known her as a friend of a friend for some time. Hmmmm, turns out Tammy lives in the same complex but no worries, she has a boyfriend. I'm done.

"My friend introduces us. I said hi, she said hi, and her boyfriend at the time was there. I thought she was drop-dead gorgeous, she was a sweet girl. But I'm done. She's got a boyfriend. Then my friend told me she and her boyfriend were having problems, he was quite the abuser. Hmmmm. Again. Hmmmm.

"About four days later, though, it's like six in the morning and I was pulling my truck out of the garage and I saw her sitting there on a rock. I drove up to her and said, 'Hi, how you doin'?' She said OK. I didn't know at the time that he had just hit her. That sixth sense thing is already there and I'm like, 'Is everything OK?' And she said, "Yeah, everything is great.' She looked over at me and said something very sweet. Tammy said, 'Now you make sure you drive safe,' because she knew I was a truck driver, and she said, 'You have a great day.'

"Now I'm thinking of stuff. It's not every day somebody goes out of their way to tell you something nice, something caring like that. I was planning to put in some overtime but at that perfect second, I got a page from my boss and he said, Alex is coming in, I don't need you today. Any other day I would have been pissed but I had talked to Tammy just seconds before, so I'm like, cool, I'm taking the day off! My hearts kinda beating funny, not bad funny kinda ha-ha funny. So I turned around and as I was coming back to park she's still sitting on the rock. So I asked her to go have breakfast. We went down the street and had breakfast.

"I'm thinking, she's a good person, she's really good people. We're talking about life in general, I'm telling her about me and she's telling me about her. She never got into any of her problems or any of the details of what he was doing to her. We got to talking about the mutual friend we have. Then I just took her home and said goodbye immediately. That was that. But that wasn't that.

"What got me was how real she was. How fun to talk with. A happy, positive, yet serious person.

"I see her a couple days after that and Saturday she comes to one of our basketball games. It was her and one of her friends, cheering us on. We just said hi and bye after that.

"A couple of days go by and once again, I was leaving for work at 6 in the morning, and, get out of here, her boyfriend is chasing her down the street, hitting her in the head! So I jump into the truck, and I'm like, 'Whoa, whoa whoa!' She's crying, she runs over to my truck. And here he comes, and I'm like, 'Whoa, stop right there.' He didn't stop, so I stopped him. I knocked him out. Something I picked up in basketball.

"So here's Tammy and she was crying, and she was bleeding from the head, so like I said, I knocked him out. I put her in the truck, took her to the hospital, they put a bandage on her head. I said, 'You can stay at my place.' She came to my place but I was thinking this isn't going to work out because he knows where my place is and he is going to come looking for her. I got a friend and said we need to get all of her stuff out. We went over to her place and got all her stuff. I went and put her over with my mom at my mom's house.

"The day we were getting her stuff, and here comes the boyfriend again. Now he has his big brother with him. Tough guy. I got into it with her boyfriend again. He got knocked out again. The brother got into it. The brother got knocked out too. Then she went in and got her stuff, brought it out to the truck, and I took it over to my mom's.

"I never let her out of my sight after that. So for the next week both of us are living at my mom's house and we start house hunting. We found a cute little apartment together. That was in Covina Hills. It was a gorgeous area back then. When we moved in together we had known each other for about two weeks.

"I just knew. We both knew. Our approach to life was the same. She wanted to work to make her life better, more meaningful. She was a Certified Nursing Assistant at a convalescent hospital and she loved her job and really loved her patients. Everything we talked about was the same. We'd start conversations the same way. The saying back then was, jinx, you owe me a Coke. God we were in love.

"Two weeks later, I got down on my knee and asked Tammy to marry me. She said, 'No doubt.' Now, that's not necessarily one of the responses you see in the fairy tales but it was perfect for me. This was at our new apartment. We had been living there five, six days. It's like 5 in the morning.

"I met her family, her mom. Her dad at the time was living in Upland. We drove up to see him. He's like, 'So where do you want to get married?' We said we wanted to keep it simple, just a few friends. And he was like, 'How many friends and family do you have?' I said, 'Well I can whittle it down to my closest friends and family. So at least on my side, I can keep it down to a few hundred.'

"We ended up getting married on a beautiful, beautiful estate in Whittier, California. It was at my aunt's. She had about five acres. It all came together in a couple weeks. Her dad and stepmom threw a really beautiful wedding. Her dad is still living. He's a good, good guy.

"Before we got married, we were talking about how many kids we wanted to have. And I'm thinking pretty conservative, so I'm like, well you know, at least 10. She's like, 'That's where we're not so alike, buddy.' "

With a sharpened pencil, Tammy was able to keep her end of the wedding invitation list to right around 100. Bob recalls the list didn't mean too much.

"We had 400 people at the wedding. It was on a Saturday. It started about 5:30 or 6 at night. It was in

September. A nice warm night in Whittier, not cold at all. The party didn't end until 2 in the morning.

"We both wrote out our vows because there was a lot to remember. It was perfect. I remember her dress. She had a big Victorian dress. It was gorgeous! What guy ever notices a dress? I do remember this much, It took seven kids to carry the train, the train behind the dress. God my wife was beautiful.

"Here I am this big basketball playing 24-year-old kid looking down into her eyes. I'm like 8 inches taller than her. When it came time to put the ring on, she put it on my wrong hand because I accidentally put the wrong hand out. You know, I'd never been married before. We did it our way. The woman was 20 years old. We were never certain of anything in life but that we belonged together forever.

"The priest says, 'I present you Mr. and Mrs. Bob and Tammy Meyers.' We went out and it was the dancing part of the wedding, and I danced with her, just me and her. Then she danced with her dad and then my dad. Then the big party after that, then Tammy and I went to change.

"During the party, the neighbor came by and asked if we could turn up the music. He heard 'Unchained Melody' by the Righteous Brothers, and the neighbor wanted us to play it again. He asked if we would play it again.

"I'd say there were about 30 of my closest cop friends who were a part of the wedding. Some cops that worked for the L.A. Sheriff's came by because it was getting to be close to two in the morning and they said we had to keep it down. But the cops in the wedding said, 'We got this.' They said, 'Oh, keep partying.'

"When I say we did things our way, I'm saying it was our way from day one. Music too loud? The neighbors ask you to turn up the music and play the song again. Police show up? They bang on the door to say have a great time. The woman had that effect on people. She sure as hell had that effect on me from the get-go. God I'm glad I knocked that guy out."

CHAPTER 3
WILLIE NELSON AND
THE GREAT COLORADO

Of all the things Tammy and Bob Meyers shared, the love of water kept coming up. They were both confirmed river rats so they figured on taking Bob's boat out on the lower Colorado River for two weeks. They jumped in a friend's RV, hooked up the boat and headed for Katherine's Landing, Then they headed south where they put the boat in at Bullhead City. Then they headed off to Needles on the boat to meet some friends. When the Meyers were left to their own devices, their friends and a great excuse for a party wouldn't be too far off.

So while they were putting in at Bullhead City the couple pulled up for some fuel and ice.

"We look over toward the right and there's this big elaborate house there," Bob recalled. "I see this guy and I said, 'Doesn't that look like Willie Nelson?' Didn't take any other push. Tammy said, 'I'm going to find out for myself.' She got off the boat, walked down the dock and through the gate. She starts waving at me, and I walked in there. What do you know, it was Willie Nelson! Here we are starting our lives together and one of the biggest entertainers, someone who really speaks to us with his music, and he's out here to say hello and wish us a great trip. Never would have happened without her.

"We knew we were soulmates. There was skepticism because they said we only knew each other for days (something like three weeks). But the friends and the majority of the family said, oh no, those two are soulmates. You can't pull them apart. Whenever any of the friends saw us, or the family, we were always together. Tammy was the only person I ever met that had the same kind of work ethic as me. She believed in time. We planned and saved and waited about a year and a half to start having kids. I think it was about 20 years in or so, people's opinions started to shift and they were saying, yeah, I guess things might work out after all.

"If I was talking to a 24-year-old kid today who wanted to know if they should jump into marriage, I'd tell them, if you know it's right, if you know it's your soulmate, go for it. Listen to your heart. Your heart will know. Had we not taken that leap of faith, who knows what my life would have turned out like? I don't know. I know Tammy made me happy. She had a wonderful heart. She was everything to me. She was my best friend, my lover, my wife."

CHAPTER 4
ERICH NOWSCH

If there was a polar opposite to Tammy Meyers with her thriving family life, constellation of friends and indefatigable work ethic, it was Erich Nowsch. At 5-foot-3 the diminutive Erich Milton Nowsch Jr. is the sort of person who might be remembered for what he wasn't rather than what he was. At age 19 he had no job, little education, and he didn't even have a driver's license. He would explain to police, "I've been meaning to go do it but that fucking book (the driver's manual), dude!"

It's easy to imagine that, except for coming to the attention of the Las Vegas community for admitting to committing a heinous killing, Erich Nowsch might never have been noticed at all.

If Erich seemed as though he had fallen through the cracks, there were reasons, not all of them of Erich's own making. His father, Erich Nowsch Sr., at 39 years of age, committed suicide in February of 2010 — almost five years to the day Nowsch, as he later confessed to police, killed Tammy Meyers. The cause of his father's death was listed by the Clark County Coroner's Office as carbon monoxide poisoning. The body was found on an unnamed road in the mountains between the Las Vegas Valley and Lake Mead. Neighbors said that there was a profound change in Erich's personality after that. He got into drugs, they said, and dropped out of high school.

Social media provides a snapshot into a young man's life who is trying very, very hard — and failing — to look like the tough guy. Erich's Instagram profile name was "Moblife18." Instagram and Facebook pages were littered with photos of him posing, smoking weed. Social media accounts linked to Nowsch have something of a theme: Erich with multiple pictures of cash and dried green leaves in plastic baggies.

If Erich couldn't see where he was heading, at least one of his friends could. In 2013, someone wrote in the shorthand of the Internet on Nowsch's Instagram: "U look like ur dad just stick to weed nothin else. I don't wanna see u struggle like he did."

It would be easy for a young man, son of a single mother, to get washed away, lost as part of the detritus of the lower rungs of society in a city like Las Vegas where seemingly everyone is on the move. But some people always seem to be looking to lend a hand, looking to help. Erich had come to the attention of Tammy Meyers. Tammy Meyers treated Erich as one of the kids of the neighborhood who seemed to float into and out of the lives of her family and the extended family that swirled around the Meyers' home.

Kristal Meyers recalled, "We first met him in 2009 or 2010 and it was on the weekend we were moving into our house. Everyone was having a balloon fight in the park and we all threw balloons and after that we didn't really talk for a while."

But Erich was a fixture at the Ansan Sister City neighborhood park just a few blocks away from the Meyers' home and the logical place for a Meyers' family outing with their dogs.

"Next time (they saw Nowsch) was with my mom at the park and that's when he pulled out weed in front of me," Kristal recalled. "My mom asked him to please not do that in front of her, and we went home and stayed there. We never had a problem with Erich at all. I knew he did drugs, but I didn't know him enough to judge him so it was all a surprise to me."

What Kristal remembers most clearly is that, from their first meeting, her mother tried to help Erich Nowsch.

"I remember one night at the park he was walking and she tried talking to him about changing his ways and getting a job and she told him to come into the house and have some dinner," Kristal said. "And she gave him a couple bucks and the next day she said to come wash the car for extra money, and he did. And that was the end of that until 8th grade. I happened to see him in the car and he waved and I waved and that was it."

But that wasn't it. When Erich's father committed suicide, Tammy Meyers was the one adult from the neighborhood who stepped forward to console Erich after his father's death.

Bob Meyers recalls that Tammy had spent "countless hours at the park consoling this boy. She was really good to him. She fed him, she gave him money. She told him to pull his pants up and to be a man."

To anyone who took a second look, it would be pretty clear that Erich was on a death spiral. His opportunities, or lack thereof, were rapidly closing in around him.

As Erich would later explain his life to police, "Well, I'm 19. I have a hard time getting jobs because of my tattoos and my hand tats and all the things I can't really close. So I've been … making music, trying to … get it to where I can self-promote myself, know what I'm saying? And get paid like that. I've been into music since 6th grade."

When asked by veteran Homicide Detective Clifford Mogg of the Las Vegas Metropolitan Police Department, Erich would explain that he wanted to be a rap musician.

"I don't know, I play games, I've been in and out of sports throughout my life," Erich told Detective Mogg. "I had a really bad troubled childhood that I went through, maybe like 16 pills a day from the age of 5 to 12. I just refused and stopped taking them."

"Troubled childhood" would be putting it mildly. According to his lawyers, when Nowsch was an infant, he was physically abused. He suffered a skull fracture at the hands of his father, who pleaded guilty to felony child abuse, according to Erich's lawyer. There was a cascading effect on the young Nowsch's life from his earliest days. It would all come out in a recorded statement to police.

Nowsch said, "There were so many (pills). I had like patch pills I put on my side; they gave me brain seizures and shit like that. Like, I don't know, Risperdal, Adderall, there's too many. It was a long time ago. I stopped at 12. I'm 19."

If Nowsch thought he would play police with a sympathy card, he didn't realize he was up against a master. Within minutes of sitting down with the outwardly defiant Nowsch for the first time, Detective Mogg, with 12 years in the homicide division and 30 years on the force would play Nowsch right into a prison cell. Within minutes of starting a videotaped conversation between Detective Mogg and Nowsch, the two had seemingly become fast friends. The detective was understanding, friendly, helpful. The detective had developed a sudden interest in tattoos. He loved underground rap music and all things Erich.

Never play the player. Good cop/bad cop? With Detective Mogg, Metro never even needed the bad cop. It was just Erich and Detective Mogg, two new friends just shooting the breeze.

Mogg: "So you're not doing pills anymore?"

Erich: "Nah. I don't do pills anymore."

Mogg: "Tell me about your tattoos. That one's kind of cool."

Erich: "Well ... first of all you're probably wondering what PFG stands for, 'cause I've got that everywhere."

Mogg: "What's that?"

Erich: "That's my rap name. Pain, Fame, and Game."

Mogg: "Pain, Fame, and Game? Nice."

Erich: "I wanted my name to be, like, meaningful, so I thought if I could somehow make initials for my name, you know, people are gonna ask me, pain, fame and game, you know? I'm gonna go through the pain living this rap lifestyle, and I'm gonna through the game, you know? And I'm gonna live the fame, you know? I thought it was kinda neat, everybody putting money, like females, dah-dah-dah."

Detective Mogg is quick to accommodate. He's so interested in Erich's tats, he takes the cuffs off Erich; after all, they're friends.

Mogg: "You'll be cool with this." [uncuffs him]

Erich: "Yeah, go ahead. That was the whole meaning of getting blessed on my arm, originally just BFG at the bottom of the arm. Originally it was a bunch of tats."

Mogg: "How much do those tattoos cost?"

Erich: "He gave 'em to me for free … I got this one, this one … Where the numbers are, that's my dad's birthday …"

Mogg: "So you don't work, what are you into now?"

Erich: "Chillin', making music, other than that I've just been smoking, chillin' listening to music."

Mogg: "Who do you rap with?"

Erich: "I rap with lot of people, honestly … I got a lot of people who want to hit tracks with me. I was gonna go to my boy's house Marcus and finish the track. I've got the hook right there on my phone, you wanna hear it?"

Mogg: "Sure."

Erich: "It's like … it's called 'This is The End' … [raps:] *This is the beginning, and that'll be the end, and when I point this … who will be my friend? 'Cause it seems like every friendship has its end. I'm looking from the outside in.*"

Those words proved prophetic. This was officially the end for Nowsch — or it would be in the next few minutes of the interview. In a police interrogation room, Nowsch had not yet been convicted of anything. He was a pretrial detainee. Nowsch was still on the outside of the state penitentiary looking in. Shovel ready, Erich was about to go to work digging his way into the penitentiary for what could be years to come.

In the few passing days between the pursuit and deadly shooting of Tammy Meyers and his sit-down with police at the Clark County Detention Center, police would charge him with an incredible case of potentially deadly bullying of a young boy.

Published reports of the day state that Nowsch was accused of holding a knife to the neck of a young boy. The Las Vegas Review-Journal reported, "At about 3 p.m. that day, police said, Nowsch approached a group of children near Alta Drive and Anatolia Lane and pulled out a knife and held it to the boy's throat.

"The boy, who is legally blind, may not have been wearing his glasses when the attack occurred, according to a police report.

"The victim told police the blade of the knife was against a vein in his neck and Nowsch had his thumb pressed against the top of the blade, according to the report, which documents the following exchange:

" 'I'm gonna slit your throat, kid,' Nowsch said.

"The victim froze and a girl with him asked Nowsch to let him go.

" 'Fuck you, you little bitch,' Nowsch said, put the knife away and walked away.'"

CHAPTER 5
'THEY STARTED FIRING, BOOM'

In the quick-to-blame, hyper-suspicious Las Vegas media environment in the days following Tammy Meyers' killing, every action the mother and her family had taken was second-guessed and somehow took on a sinister quality.

Somehow everyone forgot that Tammy Meyers, mother of four, was the victim. Why was Tammy out with her 15-year-old daughter in the parking lot of a local junior high school at 10 p.m.? The honest answer was pretty clear-cut: She was giving her daughter a driving lesson. The comments pages for newspapers and television went wild. Driving lesson? Really? "At that hour?" As if the reader was begging for a lie, as if there were legal time limits on driving lessons. The truth is Tammy had spent her early evening having dinner with her son Matthew for his 20th birthday, and so she did not have a chance to take her daughter out until later. From Tammy's perspective there was an added benefit: By the time the birthday dinner was over there were far fewer cars on the road. Kristal, very self-conscious about the nascent stage of her driving skills, would be more at ease with less traffic. The lesson would be far safer.

Johnson Junior High is right around the corner from the Meyers' home. It is just a block away from Nowsch's mother's home. Tammy and Kristal were practicing parallel parking, going through the motions of simply running and the handling of the car.

What they didn't know was that Nowsch, hidden in the darkness of the park, was watching the lesson from a distance. Instead of seeing a mother and her daughter on an innocent driving lesson in the parking lot, Nowsch thought "gang members" who had previously threatened him with harm were stalking him, according to grand jury testimony. The 5-foot-3 Nowsch was either sincerely frightened or was looking for trouble: His backpack contained a Ruger . 45-caliber autoloader with extra clips.

The iconic Colt .45 autoloader was first pressed into service for use by the American military as a result of battlefield experience in the Philippines against the Moro soldiers which began in the late 1890s. The Moro were known to regularly take to the battlefield high on a variety of stimulant drugs with a touch of opiates thrown in for good measure. Among the toughest fighters in the world, they established a reputation as deadly knife fighters and swordsmen who often stayed on their feet long enough to kill after being shot by the .38 caliber, which was the standard American pistol round at the time. John Browning's 1911 Colt .45 autoloader provided the answer. The knockdown force from the .45 was so powerful, it would lift the victim off their feet and toss them onto their backs where they were left to die. One round was generally all it took.

On that fateful evening of February 12, the big-bore autoloader wasn't enough for Erich. Nowsch had brought along extra magazines, the proverbial little guy with the big gun.

A little after 10 p.m., Tammy told Kristal her "fun time was over" and Tammy slid behind the wheel. Instead of going straight home, Tammy continued the driving lesson on the suburban Las Vegas surface streets, explaining what she was doing as they moved along, considerably below the speed limit. As fate would have it, Tammy didn't turn down the street that would send her safely home. The lesson continued for a few more blocks. In one second Tammy Meyers was simply passing along a driving lesson to her only daughter; in the next second Tammy and the Meyers family's future would take an unimaginable turn for the worse. What followed was one of the more cowardly acts against two defenseless women that has made it to the headlines in Las Vegas in some time.

Apparently, the fact that the mother and daughter were driving so slow on a virtually vacant street with ample space to navigate around them infuriated a passing driver who lacked the common courtesy to simply go around them.

Kristal said the second car seemed to come out of nowhere: "He comes up behind us really, really fast. My mom was giving me driving tips, she was showing me stuff. She was paying attention and this car comes up behind us and he almost hits the back of us. And I'm watching, and my mom's paying attention in front of us. He swerves around us and I honk the horn not knowing what to do. He swerves into the bus lane and hits our side. So she stops really hard and we didn't roll down the windows or say anything, and she said to call 911, and I couldn't concentrate. My phone was at home, dead. And so he gets out of the car and he said, 'I'm going to kill you and your daughter.' The car was hit. It wasn't hit hard but we could tell it was hit."

Tammy's maternal instincts went on high alert. She was going to do what she had to do to protect her daughter.

"She swerves around him and goes really fast to get away from him," Kristal recalled. "I kept looking back and after we turned the corner, it was terrifying to deal with such horrific things like that. We were in the wrong place at the wrong time. My mom has always kept me from those situations. I couldn't think of what to do and knowing my dad was gone …"

Terrified, Tammy covered the two or three blocks back to the family home quickly, arriving in a minute or two. Bob Meyers' 75-year-old mother and Kristal's 22-year-old brother Brandon were the only ones home.

As they pulled into the cul-de-sac in front of the family home, Tammy broke her stunned silence.

"And she says go get your brother," Kristal recalled. "She didn't say go get the gun."

With the sense of emergency building by the second, Kristal was positioned to run from the car the second it came to a full stop. Just as it did, Kristal turned to Tammy, and the mother and daughter locked eyes for the last time.

"And she said, 'I love you.' That's all she said to me."

Kristal ran inside, where Brandon was playing a video game. Insulated from the world by headphones, he was blissfully unaware of what had happened to the two most important women in his life. Kristal stormed into Brandon's room on the verge of hysteria. Brandon instantly knew something was very wrong.

"I took my headset off and said what's going on?" Brandon recalled. "And she said, 'There's trouble, trouble.' And I'm like, 'What?' She said, 'Someone is trying to hurt us.' I set my stuff down and she goes, 'Mom's outside. They said they were going to kill us.'"

In a split second, Brandon was up and running to the defense of his mother. Before he left the house he grabbed his lawfully registered 9mm Beretta pistol.

Said Kristal, "He got his gun to protect me and my mom. And when I went outside I saw a car but they didn't come down the street or anything. They told me to get in the house, shut off all the lights and bring the dogs in. So I did. And from then on they went down the street."

Kristal has replayed the scene a thousand times in her mind. She defends Brandon's decision to grab his gun, saying, "My brother was protecting us because the guy threatened our lives. That's what any normal reaction would be, to protect me and my mom, and knowing how she was protecting me, she wasn't going to let that guy come back."

In retrospect, Brandon made a smart decision to grab his gun. There was no place to hide Tammy's car, the garage was full. Seeing the car would be a dead giveaway to Tammy and Kristal's whereabouts and the would-be attacker could have been rounding the corner at any second, indeed Kristal believes he may have cruised past the corner of the cul-de-sac where the Meyers home is located. Brandon and his pistol were the only protection for his mother, his 15-year-old sister and his 75-year-old grandmother. He was protecting his family. He was going to try to hold his ground.

But when he went outside to help his mother, Tammy had a different agenda. We will never know what raced through Tammy's panicked mind, but this much is clear: Tammy Meyers never told Brandon to bring his gun, but once he was out on the sidewalk in front of the family home she demanded he get in the car.

"I told my mom to just get inside the house, get inside, and call the police," Brandon recalled. "My mom said, 'If you don't get inside the car I'm leaving without you.' She's already scared and wants away from the house. NOW."

From Brandon's perspective, he brought the gun only to protect everyone in the house. Now he can either run back inside and leave the gun in the house or he can listen to his mother's urgent demand for help.

Gun in hand, Brandon got into the car with his mother.

With Tammy behind the wheel, the pair raced back to the scene of the road rage incident.

"It's like 10:30 at night," an emotionally distraught Brandon remembered. "It's just me and my mom. So basically we pull in right here. She tells me this is where the guy confronted her and threatened her and my sister. We are back at the scene where the accident took place."

But the would-be tough guy who was willing to threaten the lives of two defenseless women is nowhere to be found. With the threat of the road rage driver diminished, Brandon's clarity returned, but he wasn't the one threatened with murder. Tammy was.

"Then right here I'm telling Mom to go home and if we need anything we can call the police," Brandon said. "And she's just completely silent. She's scared."

Still there was nothing for Brandon and his mother to do at this point.

"We turned right to head back home."

But for Brandon, a nagging sense of dread remained. While it appeared all was going well, Brandon was still on high alert: "This is the point I started getting a bad feeling."

Tammy slowly pulled the car into a right turn which would put her back on the path home. First, she would have to drive past the Ansan Sister City Park where Erich Nowsch, his paranoia redlining, sees the car he suspected carried "rival gang members" trolling, looking to kill him.

As she passed the park next to the school where she had given Kristal driving lessons just a few minutes earlier, Tammy turned right to head home. Everything changed. Tammy saw a silver car that appeared to be the one driven by the man who had just threatened to kill her and her daughter.

Said Brandon, "She starts slowing down. As they turned the corner at the park she was startled as she saw a silver car, and she starts panicking and says, 'That's them, that's them.' We stop and we are sitting right here. They are sitting ahead of us, pulled over to the curb. We actually stop and they took off.

"They were driving about 25 or 30 mph, going normal, but once they turned they booked it."

Tammy proceeded slowly. Media reports say Tammy and Brandon followed Nowsch and his driver. The truth is they followed for only a few car lengths or so and stopped. Brandon recalled his mother did not pursue.

"My mom was going about 30," Brandon said. "Then she stopped. They stopped."

Later, the world would learn that Erich Nowsch's friend, 26-year-old Derrick Andrews, was at the wheel. He drove down the street then pulled to the left side of the street then turned slightly towards the center of the street so that the car was diagonal, across what would be oncoming traffic. Tonight, the street was deserted. Andrew's move put Erich's passenger window directly open to the Meyers who are fully stopped in the street nearly a block away.

Brandon said, "Nowsch is leaning out the window… and then … they started firing, boom, shooting right at us."

Tammy was stunned.

"My mom gets down and goes, 'What is that, what was that?' " Brandon said. "And I tell her we are getting shot at. He (Nowsch) fired like 17 in total. I told my mom we need to go off, toward the street where people are."

But Nowsch and his accomplice had turned; they were headed in the direction of the Meyers home.

"She said, 'F that, we're going home,' " Brandon said. "So she reversed and we went back to that street up there. The whole concept of this was to keep them away from the house. Away from my baby sister, and away from my grandmother. That's what her thought was."

Imagine a map with streets forming a tabletop. In a tragic turn of events, Erich and his accomplice had just turned up the left leg of the tabletop. They would need to go across the table top to the right edge of the table to get home. Tammy and Brandon had just traveled up the right leg of the table top. In order to get home they would have to go to the far left part of the table. The cars raced to their destiny.

Brandon says Tammy was in full retreat at this point: "She drives forward up the street, going about 100 mph. My grandmother and my baby sister are at home. My mom did not know who this was. So they turned down that street toward our house, so she was just bookin' it. I don't know what's going on. I got brought into something that shouldn't have even happened. So here's the thing: They stopped on Alta. They weren't even coming down the street when we were coming down the street and they had a head start. So they were waiting."

In a matter of seconds Tammy pulled into the cul-de-sac where the Meyers home is situated at the end of the block.

"Boom, we turned in and we just booked it all the way to the end," Brandon said.

Tammy pulled into the mouth of the family's driveway but there was no cover. She was at the end of the dead-end street, as far as she could go. The garage was full and the couple's work vehicle was blocking the driveway.

Brandon made a dash from the front passenger seat.

"I run all the way in front of the car, slam open the driver door and grab my mom and I hear something turn right here and I turn and see headlights," he said.

Inside the home, Kristal had immediately run into the house after being dropped off minutes earlier when Tammy raced to pick up Brandon. Kristal called her father. Heart pounding, Kristal was waiting at the window and saw her mother and brother's frantic return. It's at this point that Kristal made the first nearly hysterical, static-filled cellular call to her father that would set Bob and young Robert Meyers' lives on edge and their truck in motion some 295 miles away in Kernville, California.

According to his own statement to police little Erich Nowsch, armed with his .45 autoloader and his accomplice were pulling into the cul-de-sac. At this point there was no escape from the dead-end street without passing the assailants and their gun.

As soon as Brandon saw the headlights, "I pushed her in (back into the car) and shut the door." With the killers just a few yards away on the left side of the street, there was no time to pull Tammy from the car. Brandon at least could take comfort in the fact that Tammy was protected by the steel of the car.

Brandon took cover behind a flatbed truck on the right side of the street. If they were going to come up on Tammy they would have to run past him and his fully loaded 9mm Beretta or get off a very lucky shot that would pierce the steel of the car to hit his mother.

"They started shooting at the car," Brandon said. "You never expect anyone to shoot at you. When they started shooting at us, man, I thought I was going to die. That's my train of thought. I thought I was going to die. I've never been shot at, I've never shot at someone."

Brandon started shooting.

Brandon's 9mm was blazing and his gunfire had the desired effect: as Nowsch told police, he and his accomplice thought they were attacking a vulnerable, unarmed "kid." When Brandon began firing, Nowsch and his driver wanted no part of a fair fight. They immediately threw the car into reverse and sped away. But to Brandon's utter amazement, when he turned to check on his mother in the car he found that Tammy had exited the vehicle. For the briefest of seconds, she remained standing, unsteady on her feet.

"I looked to the left," Brandon said. "My mom was standing up and then she fell down. Right at the side of the car. I ran. I put my gun on the back of the car. I grabbed my mom. I was holding her head up, telling her to keep breathing and I was screaming for help. When I was holding her, I just saw blood. It was everywhere."

Inside the Meyers' home, Kristal's cellular call to her father dropped.

"I'm looking out the window and I see my mom get shot and I see her fall and I hear, 'OH!!' " Kristal recalled. "And obviously I'm screaming and crying and the dogs are going crazy. And my grandma comes out and I'm telling her mom's been shot and she tries going outside and gunshots are still going on. And I'm trying to hold my grandmother back from getting hurt, because I have already seen my mom on the ground. After it was all done, I heard the skid from the car and my brother's on 911 and telling my mom to keep breathing and stay awake. And I was already outside and was seeing everything."

Brandon recalls, "I was holding my mom and pulled out my own phone to call 911."

As Brandon frantically searched for the wound that was causing the loss of so much blood, he remembers hoping his mother was hit in the arm, maybe the shoulder.

Indicating his mother's temple, he said, "Then I see, just this right here."

Tammy had been hit square on in the temple. A classic kill shot.

"I was yelling at the 911 dispatcher, and this lady was taking forever," Brandon said. "I told her the address like 50 times. And it took (the ambulance service) like 10 minutes to get there. So I was sitting there with my mom in pain. She was making gurgling sounds. She tried to stop, she stopped breathing and I yelled at her and she came back to it. That was the hardest thing I've ever had to go through.

"As soon as the cop got here, he was just standing there and watched me and my mom in pain. I'm just yelling at this cop, saying 'When are they going to be here? Why aren't they here?' And the cop said, 'They're coming, they're coming.' As soon as they got here all these cops got behind me and pretty much surrounded me, thinking I'm going to do something crazy. They had to pry my mom out of my hands. So as soon as they took her, all the cops pretty much barricaded me. I couldn't walk, so they helped me walk to the lawn. I laid down, punching the grass.

They told me to calm down and breathe and stuff like that."

In order to preserve the crime scene the police had to take precautions, but as an unintended result Brandon would sit, drenched in his mother's blood, for an extended length of time.

"I was out here for about 30 minutes," he said. "I had blood all the way down my arm, on my shirt. And then as soon as I got to go inside, they wouldn't let me clean my hands of course, and then I said I need to cover them before I go inside, and they wouldn't let me do that so my little sister had to see all that. As soon as I walked inside the house and she saw me soaked with all that blood she was done. My little sister just went off. And I had to have that blood on me for a long time."

Things could have been very different, Brandon said, if the assailants had "stormed the house, took me out. I'm the only one that can defend my family. If they take me out my whole family is gone. This is what I've been thinking about. My mom, my sister, my grandma and my life could have been taken out. They tried to get me and they didn't, so they got her. My goal was to pretty much have them get me, not my mom."

Sorting through everything that had happened that night, Brandon is more certain now than ever that his mother had done the right thing that night.

"I would do the same thing for my family," he said. "I would do the same thing for anyone. Get them away from the house. They didn't know where we live, and she could have gotten them away from the house but it ended up like this. They knew where we lived, and they came back here."

Of those fleeting last seconds holding his mother, Brandon said, "I've had to live with this every single day. I've had to relive what I witnessed every night. I haven't slept. I hold a lot of things in. Someday … I'm gonna break."

CHAPTER 6
BLAMING THE VICTIM

As sad as it sounds, there is a "normal" cycle of news stories that surrounds high-profile murder victims in Las Vegas. The case breaks in the mass media. Police give a somewhat sterile thumbnail of the case. Immediately friends and associates emerge to "fill in the blanks" and humanize the victim and their family. Las Vegas and the suburbs of Clark County may house 2 million residents, but the urban area is like an island. Step one foot out of the city and, with the exception of a small town here and there, there isn't another soul for a couple hundred miles. The truth is, Las Vegas is a pretty small town; if a Las Vegan doesn't know someone in town, a friend of a friend probably does.

Despite the ever-increasing circle of Meyers' friends, that context and filling-in-the-blanks is not what happened in this case. A few members of the media and then residents would savage Tammy and her family in a totally unprecedented fashion.

There were reasons. British tabloids, notorious for sensationalism, were helped along by outlandish, critical comments attributed to the lawyers for Erich Nowsch. Not one of those statement ever helped Erich's criminal case in any way. What they would do is get the attorneys' names in the paper and hurt the memory of Tammy Meyers. The drumbeat of uninformed social media posts, devoid of firsthand knowledge, filled with ignorance and self loathing, whipped each other into a frenzied pace that only served to further confuse the public. Misstatements of fact by police, such as the definitive statement that the Meyers' family car had not been struck in the unrelated road rage incident and that there was no evidence of such a collision, were simply not true. The car had been struck on the passenger side. A piece of chrome trim was missing. There were and still are silver streaks of paint in the dents on the car. Under normal circumstances, these kinds of misstatements would be a minor issue. In the firestorm of controversy surrounding this case, the oversight cast a decidedly sinister quality to any statement the Meyers family would make.

Additionally, Bob Meyers himself was responsible for fanning the flames of doubt. Bob was simply trying to protect his children from the prying microphones and reporters' calls. He made statements to the media so that his children wouldn't have to, but Bob Meyers was not even in town on the night of Tammy's killing. Absolutely everything he "knew," he knew secondhand.

Finally, Bob Meyers was undone simply by being a human being. Try as he might to stay strong for his children, he was filled to the point of breaking with a caustic mix of rage and unrelenting sorrow over the loss of his wife of nearly 25 years. It was unbearable for him. It was almost unbearable for his friends and family to watch. His children would explain that their father virtually stopped sleeping.

That was the condition that Bob Meyers was in when he was introduced to much of the world as the de facto Meyers family spokesperson.

It didn't help that the tabloid media, including the British Daily Mail, would fire up a blast furnace of misinformation, much of it quoting "a local resident" claiming inside knowledge that the murder was the result of a "drug deal gone bad" in a piece headlined "EXCLUSIVE: Was Vegas 'road rage' murder mom actually buying DRUGS from her killer? Amazing claim in case which has baffled country"

The Daily Mail's "local resident" would later admit he had no direct knowledge of anything that could support such a damning claim against Tammy. It's probably a good thing for him that Bob Meyers didn't play basketball anymore.

There are two very disparate schools of journalism in the U.K., the first ranking among the finest journalistic standards in the world today. The second, the British tabloid press, makes the National Enquirer look like a leading contender for the Pulitzer Prize.

The Daily Mail went on to break the memorable "scoop" that "Tammy Meyers was killed by Erich Nowsch in a 'prescription drug deal gone bad,' according to one man who has been pulled into the saga."

What the Daily Mail didn't know was that Tammy Meyers had completely legal access to the most powerful opioids that exist in the world today. At the time of her killing Tammy's blood-soaked purse contained a legally written prescription bottle filled with oxycodone. But the truth left a very big, very clear foot print. The prescription was more than a month old. There was only a single pill missing from the bottle. There are several facts that can be deduced from that. The obvious one is that one pill in a month does not qualify someone as an addict. The second important point is that Tammy certainly wasn't selling them — and if she was selling them, she was selling them at a rate of no more than one pill a month. Lastly, she certainly didn't need to be buying street drugs from a source as unreliable and shaky as Erich Nowsch.

Those facts notwithstanding, reporters from the Mail would pick at the smallest inconsistencies to turn the story against the murder victim.

Las Vegas is a city with some history when it comes to nefarious criminals. Few were ever painted in such a horrible light and Tammy was *the victim*.

The Mail pounded away, "The family's version of events as to how Mrs. Meyers and her armed son came to be followed back to her house and shot at by Nowsch and two accomplices has changed over the course of the last week, but many are still not satisfied the fatal shooting was provoked by a misunderstanding while she was teaching her teenage daughter to drive."

In the light of day, it raises the question: What other ways might Tammy Meyers have chosen to get herself murdered? Perhaps the family was covering up those alternate methods.

Tammy's memory would be tarnished beyond recognition. The Meyers family would endure the irresponsible, baseless rantings day after day, month after month.

It was at this point that Bob Meyers vowed he would not bury his wife until her name was cleared and she could rest in peace.

The Mail wrote: "The family remains silent on the matter, but local resident Robert Selig, 47, thinks he knows the truth after being part of Nowsch's inner circle before he was turned on and threatened by him and his friends.

"In an exclusive interview with MailOnline, he said: 'Nobody chased nobody down. The son and mother left the Meyers residence looking for Erich on a drug deal gone bad. That's the word on the street. A prescription drug deal gone bad.

'All this stuff with Mrs. Meyers, is all pharmaceutical pills and drugs. That's what Erich sold at that park. And that's why Mrs. Meyers went there, picking up pharmaceutical pills from Erich, like Xanax. The kid sold it right there at that concrete table, day in day out.' "

It sounds like absolute, verified fact, doesn't it? "The word on the street." Take it to the bank. Selig would later admit to a former veteran Metro Police officer he had no direct knowledge of any such dealings. None.

The Mail stories were probably the basis of most of the misinformation that would filter into local media stories. The Mail reported, "They (the Meyers) had initially claimed she was giving her daughter a driving lesson at night and had become embroiled in an argument with Nowsch, who had followed them home and shot at them."

Well, the Meyers never "claimed" anything. Tammy was giving Kristal a driving lesson. Period. There was no "claim". What the Meyers definitely did not say is that they became "embroiled in an argument with Nowsch." Nowsch was not involved in the road rage incident and the Meyers family never said he was. Kristal told authorities she was certain Nowsch was not the road rage driver.

The Mail continued, "It has since emerged that she had returned to her house and recruited her 22-year-old son Brandon to accompany her and look for Nowsch."

Well, they weren't looking for Nowsch because until they got to the park that had not yet encountered Nowsch that night.

That media and social media campaign against the memory Tammy Meyers, the victim of a brutal killing, was being fed in no small part by Nowsch's defense attorney Conrad Claus. Claus must have forgotten that victims' families often have a deciding voice in whether a prosecutor's office pursues the death penalty.

There is an old saying in warfare that good tactics can never repair bad strategy. The day-to-day tactics that Erich's defense team employed seemed to work for them, not Nowsch. They got their names in the paper and tormented the murder victim's family. From a long-term strategic standpoint the plan was less than stellar from day one. Upon Erich's conviction, which seemed like a dead-bang certainty, the Meyers' family would be called on, under Nevada law, to give their victims' impact statement at the time of Erich's sentencing. Bad, really bad, strategy. It was as if Nowsch's lawyers were insulting jurors and accusing them of heinous acts right before those same jurors began deliberations. Might not be the best idea.

As the Meyers' family attorney Sam Schwartz noted, "Tammy Meyers is the victim in this case. She was simply a mother trying to protect her family including her 75 year-old mother in law who was living with them. So to suggest that somehow Tammy Meyers is the bad guy here for not threatening anyone, not chasing anyone, just defending her family and getting a bullet to the head for it, I think it's incredulous and nothing short of disappointing."

CHAPTER 7
DONOR

Tammy Meyers did not die the night that she was shot. She hung on until the evening of Valentine's Day. As much as Bob Meyers was certain that deep inside, Tammy knew he was at her side, he now slowly, painfully came to terms with the certainty that the last bit of her, the last of Tammy Meyers' consciousness and connection to this world, was slipping away.

"Nobody ever left from the family, we were always there," Bob said. "Sitting in there. The nurses at UMC Trauma did an awesome job. They had her best interests at heart. They did the best job for Tammy: changing her bandages, they were there for the kids, they just did an awesome job."

Bob recalled, "There were a lot of people there. Every doctor stayed, every nurse stayed. There was a nurse working another shift off the clock; she stayed.

"Then I went back inside and I tried talking to her, because prior to that, I'd say something and she'd shake in my hand, but that day she wasn't doing it anymore. I could tell she was having a really hard time breathing. The presence in her started slipping away the next day, and it went pretty rapidly. She didn't look the same. It was really bad."

Just as Bob had come to the realization on that long hard ride back from California that his wife had suffered a terrible trauma that would take her life, he now knew that this was the time. He had to bring himself to let go and say goodbye.

"They told me what would happen and what to expect. They said the machines were keeping her alive. So it will be pretty intense, and then she'll stop breathing."

Tammy and Bob were the kind of parents who always gave the kids some say-so in how big decisions for the family would be made. Bob knew he wasn't going to put one ounce of this decision on his children.

"I just told the kids what was going to happen; I didn't ask them. I didn't want them to have that burden.

"I told the kids and everybody to get out."

The two had spent a lifetime together. From the first days of their relationship Bob knew what to do. Now sitting next to his wife of 25 years, if Tammy was going to struggle the answer was clear.

"I had to let her go. I looked at the nurse and I told her. Let her go.

"Immediately when I turned off the machine she had problems breathing.

"It took about three or four minutes, and they were the worst minutes of my life. She fought on for a few minutes and then she stopped breathing.

"Then nurses cleaned her up a little bit. I let the kids come in and say goodbye."

Bob would have to hang on for his kids. He would have to hold it together honor Tammy's wishes and would immediately fill out the required paperwork.

"She was a donor. They told me what parts could be donated and what they'll use. Then she went to that place, you know, wherever you go when you go out."

"I walked outside and I screamed. I just collapsed against the wall. It took me about 30 minutes to compose myself."

A victim's family. An organ donor who gave of herself even in death. The Meyers family would walk from the cocoon of the Intensive Care Unit into the blistering heat of a community that would savage Tammy's memory and accuse her of nearly every nefarious act imaginable.

CHAPTER 8
A MEDIA ENVIRONMENT
GONE MAD

What follows is a sampling of the mudslinging that was pursued with such vigor against Tammy and the Meyers family:

- *"Believing anything the Meyers family is saying without looking for evidence to back it up would be an unwise thing to do."* — *Nowsch defense attorney Conrad Claus, Las Vegas Review-Journal, Feb. 27*

- *"When you're trying to make sense of things, you know that Brandon Meyers hasn't told the truth."* — *Nowsch defense attorney Conrad Claus, LVRJ, Feb. 27*

- *"Exclusive: Was Vegas 'road rage' murder mom actually buying DRUGS from her killer?"* — *U.K. Daily Mail, Feb. 23*

- *"Dead woman had been buying drugs including Xanax from Nowsch says Selig, who says teenager had become notorious for dealing"* — *U.K. Daily Mail, Feb. 23*

- *"The son and mother left the Meyers residence looking for Erich on a drug deal gone bad. That's the word on the street. A prescription drug deal gone bad."* — *local resident Robert Selig, U.K. Daily Mail, Feb. 23*

- *"bitch got what she deserved"* — *Facebook user Mark-John Adam Andrew Michalikov II (likely a pseudonym), on Facebook*

- *"If the security cameras trained on the parking lot show no driving lesson, Nowsch's lawyer Conrad Claus said outside of court, 'it tends to make what they're saying a little less credible.' "* — LVRJ, March 6

- *"There have been way too many lies told by the Meyers family."* — Peter Constantine, LVRJ comments section, March 6

- *"Questions have also been raised about Meyers and her connection to Nowsch and illicit drugs."* — KLAS-TV 8 News Now, Feb. 27

- *"Got what she deserved."* — Mark Pfister (likely a pseudonym), LVRJ comments section, April 6

- *"Still sounds like a drug deal gone bad."* — Facebook user Kimberly Ann Hosfeld, on Facebook

- *"Yeah! Drug addicts all along. But to involve ur son, despicable!"* — Facebook user Betty Mency, on Facebook

- *"Another case of a drug deal gone bad."* — Facebook user Lynn Ivins, on Facebook

- *"OMG, too funny! The husband is still lying on his own Facebook page, Bob Meyers."* — "dragonsfly," LVRJ comments section, March 12

- *"The victim is guilty of the same. ... They are all drug addicts."* — James Rustler, LVRJ comments section, March 12

CHAPTER 9
CLARITY

Veteran Las Vegas Review-Journal columnist John L. Smith sat down with Bob and Brandon Meyers to clear up the widespread rumors, authoring a column on March 17 titled, "Son: Tammy Meyers was 'the mom people would want to have.' "

The column was a snapshot of the pressure to clear Tammy's name and included Smith's observation that the way "… attorneys for defendant Erich Nowsch have elbowed into the press on behalf of their client, you'd almost think Meyers was on trial. Wicked rumors and innuendo to the contrary, the 44-year-old was a victim of homicide.

"In that light, Meyers' oldest son, 22-year-old Brandon Meyers, finds himself defending his mother in death as he tried to come to her aid in life. He accompanied Meyers on the ill-fated ride-along that ended in a shootout and tragedy.

"Although not charged with a crime, in a Tuesday morning interview he clearly was shouldering the collective weight of events. It's a weight he said he'll carry a long time.

" 'What they're trying to do is they're trying to knock her down so no one feels bad for her,' he said. 'It's not right. It's not right at all.'

"Contrary to the portrait that's been painted by the Nowsch defense team, Conrad Claus and Augustus

Claus, her eldest son said Tammy Meyers was a hardworking, stay-at-home mom who kept the family together through tough times."

Finally, there was an amazing anecdote that surfaced in the Smith column, recounted by Brandon: "There was another incident a little while before this that some guy was cussing at her and calling her bad names because she was driving too slow. She was following the law. ... He was going off. He was a gang member. She followed him home. She just wanted to know why, what did I do to deserve all this? Why were you calling me all those names? Why did you say all that stuff, and why were you trying to swerve into me?

"When she spoke to him, his wife came outside and asked what was going on. And guess what happened? He apologized.

"The lady said, 'I'm sorry.' They live right down the street from us. She came to my mother's candlelight (vigil)."

Brandon continued: "She was the mom people would love to have. She took care of everyone who came around the house, kids I've never even seen before. If they needed clothes, I would have to give up my clothes. ... I made new friends just because of her. I made best friends, actually to this day because of my mom, because of the nice person she is.

"What people are saying about her is just wrong. They're saying that she was a drug dealer, that she was looking for this, that she deserved everything that she got.

"My mom didn't go looking for trouble. She keeps it away from the family. That was her goal that day, to keep it away from her family. And as her son, I didn't want her to go. I didn't want her to go by herself. She asked me ... so I went. That's the duty of being a son. You're going to protect your mother. You're going to protect your family. She did that to protect our family."

And Brandon Meyers plans to do his best to protect her memory even as he relives the events of that awful night over and over again.

Rather than seeing the clear-cut tragedy of the situation, when confronted with the truth, readers seemed to double down on their vicious, baseless comments on the Las Vegas newspaper's website that would later be proven to completely unfounded:

- *"Yeah, I remember how my Mom used to haul out and get into gunfights in a fit of pique over absolutely nothing, so this story hits close to home. I miss her role-model ways."*

- *"How much of this 'story' can we really believe? Since the whole family has proven to be liars?"*

- *"I don't want a stupid mom who looks for a fight and endanger her life and children."*

- *"I'm one of those that believes that an illegal transaction occurred earlier that evening with Tammy, her daughter and a dealer of some sort. Which leads me to believe that they got taken, wanted their funds back, dealer said no and threaten them, Mom runs home grabs son, who grabs his gun, and then the showdown with the kid around the corner occurred . . ."*

- *"Bury the bimbo, already."*

- *"This trash family is going to cost the DA his job."*

Las Vegas has a lot to be proud of: how the community has grown and matured, for example, and the way the economy rallied back from a deep recession is remarkable. But the community's reaction to Tammy Meyers' death was one of the city's darkest hours.

Of course the anonymous nature of the comments section tends to bring out the worst in people. Erich Nowsch's lawyers, however, are a completely different matter. They knew that none of the misdirection, not a word of it, was true. They had Erich Nowsch's confession in hand. Tammy's death occurred the way the Meyers family had claimed all along. Their mother was shot by a killer, plain and simple. Erich Nowsch didn't think he was killing a good mother. It was mistaken identity. Just as he had threatened to slit the throat of a small blind child in the days after he killed Tammy Meyers. Erich was just being Erich.

In what will likely live on as one of the more embarrassing moments of journalism in Las Vegas, one television station went so far as to raise the question of whether a long-estranged cousin of Tammy Meyers was the driver of the road rage car. The station enlisted the help of an identification expert to tie the relative to the driver. (Incidentally, the cousin died an untimely death by drowning in Colorado in March 2015.)

In order for the reporter to believe that as even a remote possibility, you had to believe that a long-estranged relative of Tammy's had come to town, got involved in a road rage beef with Tammy and her daughter while they happened to be out on a driving lesson, and arranged for Erich to kill Tammy Meyers within minutes. Tammy would have to forget what her relative looked like, or at least not mention that fact to her daughter Kristal or her son Brandon. Perhaps the reporter, his editors and fact-checkers had overlooked the fact that Erich Nowsch had *confessed* to shooting the mother of four in a case of mistaken identity. The news report was one of the low-water marks in Las Vegas journalism on the case.

Bob Meyers summed it all up, the horrible positions, the supposition and character assassination that Tammy was saddled with: "My wife, she was a firm believer in forgiveness, but I can't tend to want to forgive the people who have said the hateful things they've said and there's been a bunch."

Brandon Meyers would add, "Strangers who have never even met her, never had a conversation with her, had never even seen her before other than this incident, yet they still have things to say about her."

That truly was the dividing line. The hateful nasty things that were so quickly volunteered against Tammy universally came from people who *had never met her.* People who knew Tammy Meyers had nothing but glowing praise for her.

Said Tara Estes, "If you needed her and it was 3 o'clock in the morning you would just call her. You would call her crying and she would be, 'OK, be at my house, I've got the ice cream. Let's talk.' She just wanted to be everyone's mom and friend."

Estes is one of the young women the family has always referred to as "Tammy's Girls."

When Tammy came under cyber-attack shortly after her murder, "Tammy's girls" immediately came forward to team up, to do their best to set the record straight about the woman who had done so much to help people without ever asking for anything in return.

"She was the sweetest person you could ever meet. A great mom, friend, best friend, all around great person," remembered Nichole McLaughlin.

Amanda Ahlstrom says Tammy's heart was wide open: "Any problem that you had or any doubt that you had about your life she would be there to help you through it and I think that's what was so special about her. You don't meet many people who care enough, even if she didn't know you. She still cared."

One of "Tammy's Girls," McKenzie Webster said: "You didn't have to know her long before you knew she was special. It was instant comfort she gave you."

Kristal Meyers, in a halting, quiet voice, tried to tell those who were so quick to judge that her mother was an exceptional person: "She was always there for everyone; she never doubted anyone. And what people say about my mom, I know it's not true because they've never met her before. How do they know what she's like? You literally have to meet my mom to know what she's like. And everyone who knows my mom and meets her loves her to death, and no one who has met her has ever said anything bad about my mom."

Robert Meyers Jr. said it was Tammy's gift that people instantly felt at home with her: "Everyone always called her mom. She's been there no matter what. If they were going through a hard time, going through bad times like girls breaking up with their boyfriend they'd come over and mom used to talk with them for hours. My mom was that loving caring person that everyone needed."

Her son Matthew remembers a time the family was out on the road and were beyond hungry. They finally pulled into town and found an In-N-Out Burger. Great food. Not the fastest fast food in the world, so the hungry wait seems like forever.

Matthew recalled, "A little girl and her mom came up. The little girl was about five. The little girl asked her mother 'Mom, can you get me some food?' and her mom answered that they didn't have enough money." Tammy grabbed her own food, Matthew remembered: "The fries, the food, the drink that she got, and she gave it to the family."

Giving up an In-N-Out Burger is where many of us lesser beings might otherwise draw the line.

Matthew said, "There were always 20 of our friends coming over for Thanksgiving, Christmas; it didn't matter if it was just for family."

Bob recalled the times Tammy volunteered for all kinds of work: "She said we're going to the Boys & Girls Club. She said we're going to become members. I said, 'We are? Aren't we a little old?' And she said, 'No, we're going to become members and we are going to help them out down there.' They don't have a football program. Six teams. She did it all, every team, every age group."

Matthew says when it came to being a mom, Tammy was a natural.

"We called her 'Momma Bear,' everyone's mom," he said. "Any kid that didn't have a mom? That was like their mom."

So that's the person who was the focus of so many cheap shots on the threads in social media. She is the one for whom "the word on the street" was so twisted and cruel. The writers who wrote such terrible things just didn't know. It makes you wonder how many of them went out of their way to help the homeless, to stay up to console a friend, to prepare elaborate holiday dinners for children who otherwise would have spent the day alone. Those cheap-shot artists just didn't know.

But Erich Nowsch's lawyers knew the truth. They knew Nowsch didn't even know he was killing Tammy Meyers. Nowsch thought he was shooting "a kid," a rival gang member.

Even though Tammy was a huge proponent of work, who thought a job and some hours on the clock could straighten out just about anyone's problems, she had no criticism for unemployable, completely unmotivated Nowsch, who was so lost in life. She took the time to counsel him.

Matthew recalls Tammy trying to help Erich, telling the young man who would later become her killer, "Go back to school, finish school."

Matthew said of Nowsch: "He hung out with the wrong kids and those kids were always the kids involved with drugs or who wanted to fight."

The savagery on Facebook and in the comments section of the Las Vegas newspaper took Bob Meyers Sr. completely by surprise. As much as anything, that kind of cruel, completely unfounded criticism of his wife was what was keeping Bob Meyers awake at night.

"It's like the killer is the victim here," Bob said. "He's not the victim. I'm a miserable wreck. There is nothing that is going to replace what I lost. I'm not getting through it. You can't get through it. My best friend, my lover, my wife is gone. What's there to get through? I look over to the side of the bed when I go to sleep. We always said, 'I love you, I love you back, I love you more.'"

For Bob Meyers it was like the nightmare wouldn't end and the pit truly had no bottom.

Said Kristal, "Our family is trying to stay strong, and trying not to think about all the bad stuff and all these rude comments that people are saying. It's not going to tear us down; it's going to make us keep growing stronger, something my mom would want us to do. My mom loved everyone; she wasn't this bad person."

Erich Nowsch didn't just kill a mother of four. He killed a person who was a surrogate mother to dozens, perhaps more than a hundred young people. Those social media posts so casually thrown around were aimed a woman who would have taken any one of those malcontent writers into her home. That who she was. That's who they are.

Kristal Meyers said there is only way to fully understand just the kind of person her mother was: "I really wish you could have met her."

CHAPTER 10
COMING CLEAN

By the early morning hours following the shooting of Tammy Meyers, Erich Nowsch had sealed his fate. The night had been too much for one person to absorb. He turned to Khatelyn Krisztian, his closest friend, someone he felt would understand him and help him to put the shooting in perspective.

At this point Erich had no idea who he had shot or if had even actually hit someone that evening. While Tammy Meyers' heretofore impeccable reputation was being dragged through the mud by would-be moralists wildly speculating about an illicit relationship between Erich and her gone bad, their "word on the street" had no basis in reality whatsoever. Erich bragged to his friend Khatelyn he thought he had "shot a kid." Those who had said such horrible things about Tammy in the weeks to follow did so out of a malignant ignorance.

On the other hand Nowsch's attorneys, who fed the flames of that ignorance in attacking the victim and the tormented family, knew exactly what they were doing when they tried to damage the reputation of the innocent woman.

Khatelyn Krisztian had known Erich for about a year and a half. The two were very close. Questioned by David Stanton, Chief Deputy District Attorney of the Clark County District Attorney's Office, she would testify before the Clark County Grand Jury on

March 5, just 24 days after Tammy's shooting, that she and Nowsch were like "brother and sister."

The exchange started a few hours after Tammy Meyers had been shot. Khatelyn and her boyfriend, Zack, received a text from Nowsch. It was a little before 3:33 that morning of the 13th. Khatelyn testified that Erich texted, "That he had to come over, there was something important."

By 4 a.m. Erich was knocking at her door with a black backpack in hand. Khatelyn testified the first thing out of her friend Erich's mouth was, "I got them."

According to Khatelyn's sworn testimony before the grand jury, Erich had told her, "He (Erich) was in the park and there was a car in the school parking lot which is near the park. He saw the car, thought that it was after him, looking for him, waiting for him. At that point he called a friend to pick him up. The friend came and picked him up. They stayed in the same vicinity, the neighborhood of the park area. At that point either they had gone into the school parking lot or just out of it, but at that point there was some type of meeting or encounter. And he didn't express that words were shared, but that the vehicle came after him or he came after the vehicle. Also shared that there was a gun being waved out of the car, didn't specify what window. At that point he sees a gun, pulls his gun out and fires. He didn't say how many shots. And then the car, again I'm not sure who's following who, but they came around a corner, ended up in the cul-de-sac and at that point fired again several times. He says that 22 shots went off altogether."

For anyone keeping score, it's official: Erich's life as a rapper and unemployable street kid is over. He admitted to his best friend that he killed Tammy Meyers, and she just put it on the record for law enforcement.

Erich's friend knew him well enough to doubt just about anything he said. Prosecutor Stanton asked Khatelyn, "At that time you thought he was exaggerating?" Khatelyn was quick to answer, "Very much so." But it is at this point that Nowsch goes to his backpack to show Khatelyn and Zack the weapon that, according to a later statement to police, he used to shoot Tammy Meyers squarely in the temple.

Nowsch had the three magazines and the gun in his backpack just as he had in the shooting a few hours earlier. He laid it all out to Khatelyn and her boyfriend. His explanation in no way resembled the sordid, twisted story that had so firmly captured some Las Vegans' prurient interests. No drug deals with Tammy. No "relationship gone bad." Not one word of that utter bullshit was true, according to the only person who truly knew his motivation.

Bottom line: Erich Nowsch shot Tammy Meyers to death in a case of mistaken identity.

Prosecutor Stanton asked, "Did Mr. Nowsch describe in his description of what happened earlier that night or morning an event where he confronted a mother and a daughter in a car?"

Khatelyn: "Not at all."

Prosecutor Stanton: "Now he describes to you the cul-de-sac incident and you said that he fired, or told you that he fired in excess of 20 times. Did he tell you about what he was observing and who he was firing at in the cul-de-sac?

Khatelyn: "The only description I have of that is they pull into the cul-de-sac, shots go off at the vehicle. At that point someone — not male, female, tall, short, no description — gets out of the car and runs towards the front door. At that point he shoots, firing shots at the door, and then once that threat I guess was gone in the house, shoots at the car again and that was the end of it."

Earlier Khatelyn had told police in detail all about Nowsch's story recalling that he told her, "I know I hit somebody but I don't know if they're dead. I don't know what injuries but I know I hit somebody. I know somebody's hit."

Prosecutor Stanton recalled that conversation that Khatelyn had shared with police: "Once again he says, once again you're paraphrasing from Mr. Nowsch to the detectives, quote, 'I don't know if they're dead. I don't know if they're injured. I don't know who it was, but I know I hit somebody.' "

Khatelyn: "Yes."

At this point of Erich's visit to her apartment on the early morning of the 13th, Khatelyn had to leave for work. It was now approaching 6:30 a.m. She and her boyfriend Zack had a private conversation outside of

Erich's presence and made a quick decision to get Erich out of their apartment as soon as possible.

Later that day Nowsch would ask Khatelyn to keep a close eye on any media accounts regarding gang shootings. Erich suggested they focus on the local Fox station.

Prosecutor Stanton: "Did you go on Fox's website?"

Khatelyn: "I did."

Prosecutor Stanton: "What were you looking for?"

Khatelyn: "A gang shooting. A kid shooting kids."

Prosecutor Stanton: "And just to paraphrase, you tell me if I'm right or wrong, 'hey, I can't see anything what you're talking about.' Is that what you kind of told him?"

Khatelyn: "Yes."

Khatelyn said Erich's response was simple. "Keep looking. Try this, try that."

Nothing seemed to fit until a friend of Khatelyn's and Zack's brought up the subject. "Aaron mentioned in conversation that he heard of an article that sounded like that," Khatelyn said.

Prosecutor Stanton: "And what did you do after you had this discussion with Aaron?"

Khatelyn: "The following day at work Zack found an article that matched Aaron and Erich, sent me the link, and I hadn't even gotten halfway through the article before I ran out of my office and called the police."

Prosecutor Stanton: "When you read this article, what is the article talking about?

Khatelyn: "Tammy Meyers."

Prosecutor Stanton: "That Tammy Meyers, a mother, had been shot in the head or shot in a shooting that occurred the evening of the 12th?"

Khatelyn: "Yes."

Prosecutor Stanton: "I think you said you are not even halfway through the article and the details in that article are now matching up to what?"

Khatelyn: "Exactly what Erich described."

Prosecutor Stanton: "And you said that you're at work when you're reading this?"

Khatelyn: "Yes."

Prosecutor Stanton: "What did you do when you read not even halfway through the article?"

Khatelyn: "Ran out. Got up, told the receptionist I'll be right back."

Prosecutor Stanton: "And then you ran outside of the building ... and who did you call?"

Khatelyn: "Crime Stoppers."

Prosecutor Stanton: "And you reported this to the police?"

Khatelyn: "Yes."

What Khatelyn didn't know is that at almost that same precise moment, her boyfriend Zack was making that same call to turn Erich in to the police.

Police had known the very day after Tammy died exactly who her killer was and that it was a case of mistaken identity. At the very latest, Nowsch's attorneys would know after they signed on the case and got the grand jury transcript.

Despite knowing exactly what had happened to Tammy, Nowsch's lawyers left the innocent murder victim and her family to twist in the wind while they fanned the flames intended to consume what was left of Tammy's reputation.

One of Nowsch attorney Conrad Claus's more infuriating statements suggested that there was ongoing interaction between Nowsch and Tammy — and potentially funds being exchanged.

While technically true, that statement was sickeningly misleading. It was clearly intended to leave the door open to the possibility that Tammy had some nefarious relationship with her killer.

The truth is there *were* interactions going on between Tammy and Erich. Just as she did with "Tammy's Girls," Tammy had done everything she could to console Erich after his father committed suicide. Years later when he continued to fail in school and further fail in life she saw him as a lost young man and fed him, mentored him and gave him money. She told him to go back to school. Those were the "interactions;" those were the "funds."

Given the context of the wildly inaccurate rumors of the time, Claus was one of only a handful of people who were in a position to absolve Tammy Meyers of these imaginary indiscretions without doing an iota of damage to his client's case. He chose to cast further doubts on the victim, knowing full well that Erich Nowsch had confessed to killing Tammy Meyers in a case of mistaken identity.

As Erich explained to police: "I'm so sorry. Just tell them that my intentions were to take someone bad out, not a loving, caring mom."

That was the difference between Erich and his attorneys, as far as reputation was concerned. A loving, caring mom was exactly who the attorneys intended to "take out."

CHAPTER 11
BUSTED

Erich knew police were onto him. They had spoken to him just five days after the shooting. He had an unrelated, outstanding warrant. That first encounter was when he first started lying to police regarding his whereabouts the night of Tammy's killing. He claimed he was at a friend's recording studio. His friend was quick to set the record straight: Erich wasn't there that night.

It was a Thursday at about 1 in the afternoon when the brief standoff started. Television crews and newspaper reporters started pulling into the normally quiet neighborhood which is about 12 miles west of the Las Vegas Strip, about one block from the Meyers home. As one media report described the scene, it "played out like something from a movie, with SWAT teams and a helicopter to flush the 5-foot-3, 19-year-old boy from his home."

The Los Angeles Times reported: "A neighbor of Nowsch told TV news that she heard police over a loudspeaker telling him to come out of the house with his hands up or to at least come to the window so police could see that he was not harmed. His mother said he had threatened to shoot himself."

In all, the standoff lasted a little more than an hour. The junior high school down the street had to be locked down for the duration of the police operation. Erich's mother, Kathleen Babin Nowsch, called police before things got too real. Had things escalated,

SWAT generally uses tear gas to clear a home. The tear gas canisters have a nasty habit of catching fire and burning buildings to the ground because firefighters can't rush into a burning building until police have cleared it.

In this case Erich did as he was told, came out, dropped his cell phone (which would prove so valuable to sealing his fate), and police rushed in to take Erich Nowsch away for what would probably be years.

In a mixture of rage and relief that his wife's killer was finally apprehended, Bob Meyers exploded in front of the media, shouting at reporters: "There's the (expletive) who killed my wife. Are you all happy? You made my wife look like an animal, and my son. There's the animal."

Nowsch had been under surveillance since the day after the shooting, when his friend Khatelyn Krisztian, who later testified before the Clark County Grand Jury, had advised police of Erich's role in the killing.

This was one of the other areas that would lead members of the media and the community to turn against the Meyers family. After telling police about Erich's role in the killing, Krisztian was told to hold the information in the strictest confidence. People are people. She told at least one friend and, well, people are people. That friend immediately told the Meyers family that police were on to Erich and had him under surveillance.

On the day of Erich's arrest, Bob Meyers informed the media that the family "knew all along" that Nowsch was the killer. Members of the media were rightly stunned. How did Bob Meyers know the killer? What was going on? Were all the rumors true after all? Why hadn't police been informed that Meyers knew Nowsch? The rumor mill went into overdrive.

The answers were pretty simple. Khatelyn Krisztian wasn't supposed to tell anyone that Nowsch had confessed to her and that she had informed police. Nowsch obviously knew where the Meyers family lived. Lives could be in danger. When Meyers heard it from that mutual friend of Krisztian who lived in the area he didn't want to get Krisztian in trouble, nor did he want to jeopardize the investigation. From the Meyers family's perspective it was innocent enough. From the media's perspective, well, it looked pretty hinky. Without meaning to, in a moment of understandable rage Bob Meyers had raised another red flag, another giant question mark over the Meyers family's account of how Tammy came to be killed.

Ironically, it would be Eric Nowsch who would absolve Tammy of any supposed involvement in her death with his complete confession to the killing.

CHAPTER 12
CONFESSION

It didn't take long for Metro Homicide Detective Clifford Mogg to let Erich in on a little secret: They had him. Police could prove Nowsch was lying. One second Mogg was Erich's friend, anxious to learn more about Nowsch's fascinating life as an unemployable rap star; the next moment, Erich knew the wheels had come off. One second Erich was denying his involvement, the next second he was explaining the killing. On the tape, Nowsch is shifting gears mentally. His speech changes from fairly straightforward English to … not English.

Nowsch: "I swear I thought they was gonna pop all of you, bros. They went past my house. [Unintelligible] … I knew I saw a gun, bros. I knew I saw a gun aimed at my house, dude. I didn't mean to hit no mom, bros. Nobody's mom."

Detective Mogg: "Tell me what happened, from the beginning."

Nowsch [crying]: "Look, man. I'm having a hell of a threat. So I got this gun, and I was at the park. Every direction, she was just following."

Detective Mogg: "Who?"

Nowsch: "Whoever was driving the car. We're on the same page, being honest. The green car, the one she was in. I'm gonna be honest now."

Detective Mogg: "I'm glad you're gonna do this. Perfect. Go ahead. Tell me."

Nowsch: "So every time I was moving, I'd go right, go left, go behind the bush, I'd exit toward the park, I'd exit the this way. Every way I went, that car was there. And I just had threats that morning on the phone ... they was gonna pay me a visit. It's no joke. They pay visits, they don't leave until there's bodies. So I got frightened, I got the gun. I already had multiple threats from different people for reasons I can never tell you. The thing with Stan [a person in the neighborhood] was, the dude owed me money. I took like eight of his plants out of his back yard. He got them back the next morning. He been trying to get me arrested, killed ever since. Had people threatening my life, talking about they're gonna skin my cat, skin my baby sister, my mom. They always wanted to drive a car like my mom's. All this shit. I got scared. I lost my dad, man, I can't lose my mom. Or my baby sister, who doesn't even have a father.

"It's just, every direction I went, she was there, dude. Like there was no questions, I pulled that bitch out, I cocked it back, I did it like three times, I took it out of the chamber ... she'll be back out in the parking lot. I was supposed to meet up with these girls, I completely blew them off 'cause I thought they were in danger. I didn't want to hop in their car ... we went at it for a minute, they just didn't leave the road, dude, like they knew what they were doing the whole time. It was 30-45 minutes before I even got in a car, it wasn't right, like they were following me for so long. They were waiting for me to get into a car. I didn't want to get in his car at all, until I knew this car was out of sight and they weren't watching me anymore ...

"I got in his car and they just came out of nowhere. This shit went down, got to chasing them for like 20 minutes, and fucking, we were gonna leave and shit, and then, we were already to leave and wahhh, they hit the fucking corner. And fucking, they were right behind us, and they followed us. They followed us. My boy was like, they gonna play this game. ... It was so convincing dude. They were following us, and they didn't even turn. I held my pistol out the window like this, like a huge warning."

Detective Mogg: "Did you shoot?"

Nowsch: "No, I just held it out. And they just fucking kept following us all the way down the road. I was like, they're gonna bust on us, dude. And I just cocked it back and I started shooting on them. I held it out the window and they kept following. And I saw more than one or two people in that car. I knew I was gonna get shot, I thought it was going down. I didn't feel there was anything I can do. They keep threatening my family, dude. They can kill me but don't go for my family. You see what I'm saying? You're not gonna hurt me by hurting me, but you're gonna hurt me if you hurt my family.

"And it wasn't intentional, dude, when I found out I fucking bawled, man."

Detective Mogg: "After you shot, what happened then?"

Nowsch: "When he shot the first time, I shot, it kind of went in reverse, and they stopped. We started off. I got to thinking, like no, hell, no, I was like, this ain't right at all. [Long pause.] Man, what I'm doing, I'm gonna get my mama killed, bro. Y'all can't let my mama get killed. People are gonna go for her, y'all don't understand."

Detective Mogg: "No."

Nowsch: "When they find out it was me, man, so many people, bro."

Detective Mogg: "Listen. After the first time, what happened then?"

Nowsch: "I shot off ... all I could keep thinking was, I didn't hit them."

Detective Mogg: "The first one, where was that?"

Nowsch: "The street."

Detective Mogg: "Let me draw it for you."

Nowsch: "I didn't think I hit him, so we left. We were gone. I was like, no, dude, we gotta go back, I didn't hit him. ... They're gonna go toward my house. So sure e-fucking-nough, dude, it got more and more convincing to me, man. We go up towards fucking Cimarron, man. [Unintelligible] ... I didn't give a fuck what he said, I was like, we're going back dude. We go back, and they're fucking passing my house, dude. With their arms out and everything. They're passing my house. And I just blacked. I blacked the fuck out. When they stopped pointing, whatever, I just let the whole clip."

Detective Mogg: "Where did that happen?"

Nowsch: "Right at the cul-de-sac."

Detective Mogg: "What did you see when you turned down the cul-de-sac?"

Nowsch: "We didn't go into the cul-de-sac. We were at the end of the cul-de-sac. I had my arm out the window and I was shooting. We ain't got out the car, none of that. We never hopped out the car. I was scared, like this was defense, not getting out the fucking car, man. … They still lived back there, for one. And two, why would you drive past my house and not go home? That was my first impression, that was when I think I actually hit somebody. It all seemed so real, like it was the people watching my house. And the next day those Mexicans rolled up on me, and they're threatening my mom and little sister."

Detective Mogg: "Were you guys out on Durango following this car?"

Nowsch: "I don't know, maybe. I really thought these were the guys who were threatening me the whole time, and they finally caught me slipping, is all I could keep thinking. Once they get me, they're gonna take my mom, my family, out."

Detective Mogg: "When you pulled in the cul-de-sac what did you see?"

Nowsch: "One car door opened, driver's side. I kept thinking I hit the bastard. First thing I see him running up to the door, I'm thinking they're going to grab more straps. I done let every bullet I had in there."

Detective Mogg: "Did you reload?"

Nowsch: "One clip."

Detective Mogg: "So you reloaded a clip?"

Nowsch: "Yeah. I had three clips, man. That's how scared I was of this shit. These people who are threatening me are no joke, they are everywhere, dude, they're in prison, all that. I just wanna talk to my mom."

Detective Mogg: "Could you see the person in the driver's seat?"

Nowsch: "I couldn't see nobody, I just saw heads in there. There was a dude in the passenger seat ... [unintelligible] ... I was like, fuck this, this has got to be the people. They turned, man, they ended up behind us, and we all made eye contact with each other. And it was hella sketch. You could tell it wasn't right."

Detective Mogg: "You said there was a time delay between when you saw this car kind of following you around at the park. What kind of car were you in?"

Nowsch: "I can't say, dude. I'm just speaking for my
…"

Detective Mogg: "And this was a friend of yours?
Associate?"

Nowsch: "No, a friend of a friend. Anonymous,
anonymous. I can't speak for nobody else, dude. This
shit is hard for me, bro. This was not supposed to
happen, bro. You know, like, you don't understand. I
took out the wrong person, dude. That's why they're
hella pissed. This makes sense. That's why they're so
mad."

Detective Mogg: "Who is so mad? Who did you take
out?"

Nowsch: "This is a setup, bro."

Detective Mogg: "Who did you take out, Erich?"

Nowsch: "This is a setup. Look, guys, could you like
tape what I'm saying? 'Cause I'm like really brilliant."

At this point Erich has completely confessed to one
of the highest profile killings in Southern Nevada in
years and he has just now figured out, in a police
interview room, face to face with detectives, that he
has been "set up."

Detective Mogg: "Yeah. What's the mom's name?"

Nowsch: "Tammy."

Detective Mogg: "Had you been over there for dinner or something?"

Nowsch: "Yeah.

Detective Mogg: "So you know the family."

Nowsch: "I know the whole family, man. Dude, trust me, I didn't mean to hit somebody I cared about, bro. Look man, these Stan guys, man, they're gonna, they know."

Detective Mogg: "Nobody is gonna bother your mom and your sister."

Nowsch: "They are though."

Detective Mogg: "Who do think is going to do that?"

Nowsch: "They were following me, there was no question. That car was on my shit that night. I don't care if she was teaching her to drive or not. I don't know, but they were following, they were watching, all of that. My whole thing is, Stan and them know, Robert and Brandon and all them, they talked to them to have them watch me to see if I had the balls to do that shit. If I had the balls to actually shoot or not. And so, when I did that, they saw I wasn't playing, and they got aggressive, real aggressive real quick. Hence the reason they ran out on me, hence the reason they came to my door, aggressive, why they filed a police report. They got friends in prison so they gonna see me when I go in."

Detective Mogg: "Erich. After the shooting in the cul-de-sac, were you driving?"

Nowsch: "I was in the passenger seat."

Detective Mogg: "Front, back?"

Nowsch: "Front."

Detective Mogg: "Was the window …"

Nowsch: "Down."

Detective Mogg: "Do you know how many shots you fired in the cul-de-sac?"

Nowsch: "I fired the whole clip."

Detective Mogg: "The whole clip?"

Nowsch: "I just wanted to hit them. I didn't want them to come by my house no more."

Detective Mogg: "Did anybody shoot back at you?"

Nowsch: "I'm not a killer, bro. I just, bros, like, I don't know, I blacked out, bros. My first instinct, these are the people threatening my family's life. This is my time, this is my chance right now to get rid of them. Contacting the police wouldn't do anything. … They're smart, they're gonna lay low. When the case gets closed because there's so much else going on, is when they're gonna strike. There's no winning. There's no winning, dude. There's just no winning, bro."

Mogg had left out a few other details. Because they had Erich's phone they had a pretty good idea of the identity of the driver of the silver Audi who shuttled Erich from the scene of the first shooting near the park to the scene of the deadly shooting in front of the Meyers home. Twenty-seven-year-old Derrick Andrews would allegedly be given several opportunities to help police build their case against Erich. The problem for Derrick was that police had the phone records. Police could use those records to tie him to the scene of the killing.

Like Erich, Derrick would be charged with murder, attempted murder, and conspiracy to commit murder with the use of a deadly weapon. As Clark County District Attorney Steve Wolfson would remind the media, "If you're a getaway driver, aiding and abetting another to commit a crime, you're equally guilty." In the movies the tough guy finds a way out. But the problem for Derrick was in the movies the cops don't have the cell phone and the records. In the movies the tough guy is out by the time the screen credits run at the end of the movie. In real life in Nevada the tough guy gets out after most of us have died of old age.

Nowsch had some other issues to deal with. He also faced charges of battery with use of a deadly weapon and child abuse or neglect with use of a deadly weapon for allegedly threatening to slice the throat of the small 13-year-old legally blind boy three days after he shot Tammy. These things can add up.

CHAPTER 13
ERICH: NO DEAL

Just as young Erich Nowsch had predicted, it turns out there was no winning. Bro. Erich tried to work the wrong guy. It was looking more and more like Detective Mogg had expertly used little Erich's own volunteered words to escort the confessed killer to the gates of the Nevada State Prison system for years to come.

All that remained were a few details. First among them, a hearing on whether to exclude the confession that Mogg had so expertly extracted. Nowsch's lawyers would claim Erich was too high on drugs on the day of his confession to know what he was doing when he talked to police. As if there are drugs that convince you to falsely detail your involvement in the killing of an innocent woman.

Clark County District Judge Michael Villani saw through that and ruled jurors were entitled to hear the statement at trial. The judge's decision was a trigger for a number of events. A conviction on an open murder charge could leave Erich open to the possibility that he might never spend a single living moment outside the walls and concertina wire of the Nevada State Prison system.

By the dog days of summer 2015 the last hurdles to a possible plea arrangement were in the air. There were rumors that Erich and his attorneys were in favor of taking the deal. Just rumors.

Without a plea Erich, who not only admitted that he killed Tammy Meyers but was also charged with threatening to kill a small blind child by slitting his throat, could end up spending the rest of his life in prison if convicted. The reality, not the fairly tale version that appeared in the inane social media posts, could steel jurors to help send Erich to the maximum sentence under the law. It appeared his attorneys had tried to get the community to despise Tammy. If they went to trial, those feelings of antipathy might well be erased after the first five minutes of the prosecutor's opening statement. Erich could be easily portrayed as a callous criminal. With cold hard facts on the table, not blind supposition, it would be a far easier call. In his explanation to police, Erich told police that he shot Tammy to death because he thought he was killing a gang member who had come to get him. He would have a tough time explaining what threatening gang he thought the little 13-year-old blind child belonged to.

The deal was for both Erich and Derrick to plea or both to go to trial. The district attorney's rationale: If you have to have a trial for one, might as well have a trial for both.

In the hot September days following Labor Day, deadlines for plea deals came and went. From the Meyers family's perspective, it was as if the case was a giant glacier moving at a maddeningly slow pace. There was one positive development: Social media posts in favor of the diminutive killer, the thoughtless speculation as to Tammy's involvement with her killer, came to an abrupt halt the moment Erich's full confession to the killing was made public. When someone did venture an unkind word, they got slapped down for blaming an innocent woman.

Had Erich's attorneys resorted to their tired attempts at misdirection and blaming Tammy, they would have been laughed out of the building in light of Erich's admissions.

Seven months after Tammy Meyers' murder, her family was still waiting for some closure, some modicum of peace. Bob Meyers had suffered a setback when his RV dedicated to his sales business was rear-ended in an accident on the highway. Robert Meyers Jr. had to return to a regular job while he waited for the RV to get back up and running.

Fifteen-year-old Kristal was perhaps the hardest hit of all. She had left town to get some distance from all of the reminders of that night. When she did return to town she refused to leave the house except for the briefest of moments. The stress showed on her face. There was the will to rise above it all but it was pushed down by the burden of all that she had lost and all that had been so unkindly said about her and her family.

Brandon was finding it difficult to return to his life. He rarely left home. It was not easy to process all that he had seen, heard and been accused of on that night.

Since so many have offered their opinions on how the family had behaved on the evening of Tammy Meyers' death, perhaps there is room for one more observation about Brandon Meyers and his reaction on that night. One would hope there would be one thing that might have been done differently by Brandon Meyers. Faced with a similar situation, forced into an unimaginably difficult situation, forced into a gun fight by a killer, forced to see what he saw, perhaps there is room to not be so hard on oneself. Maybe there would be a place to realize we are only human and that Brandon did the very best thing he could that night. That's all any of us can do.

If it sounds like the family remains in a defensive and reactive posture and caught up in a loop without end, ask yourself: What would you have done if your family member, such an exceptional family member, had been killed in cold blood only to be savaged by the community you called home?

The one positive outcome of a plea is that the appeals process shuts down. The killers have to admit their guilt and state for the record that they are freely and without coercion entering into the agreement. There would be no need for testimony or cross examination. With a plea deal, Erich and Derrick would just disappear and start their lives in prison.

But that's not what happened. Late on the morning of September 14, 2015, both sides, spurred on by no-nonsense District Court Judge Villani, had come to the conclusion that it was time to move on to trial. There would be no plea.

Closure for the Meyers family and all concerned would have to wait. The trial was tentatively scheduled for October 19, 2015. There would be testimony and cross examination. In some ways the Meyers family would relive the murder of Tammy all over again. But at least there would not be the absurd social media traffic claiming Tammy had somehow played a role in her own killing. To his credit, Erich Nowsch had manned up and admitted his role to police. Anyone who could read English would know there was no "drug deal" and there was no affair. The only money that had changed hands was a few dollars that were freely given in an attempt to help Erich grow up and be a man. The incendiary social media posts, promulgated by Nowsch's criminal attorneys, that had struck out against the Meyers family with the explosive, lasting impact of a sniper's bullet would begin to fade in time. No longer would family members have to read the sadistic statements like, "Bitch deserved it."

Deserved what? Deserved to have her sons and daughter grow up without her loving guidance? Deserved to leave her husband of nearly 25 years without a loving partner? Deserved to be the source of anguish for hundreds, literally hundreds, of friends who would mourn her memory for the rest of their lives?

No one, least of all Tammy Meyers, deserved that.

END BOOK ONE

ABOUT THE AUTHOR

Mark Fierro spent 10 years as a courthouse and crime reporter at KLAS-TV, the CBS television news station in Las Vegas, during an era in which organized crime exerted an intense influence in the city. Fierro went on to serve as a communications consultant in the House of Representatives on Capitol Hill. Fierro later orchestrated the messaging behind $4.5 billion in IPOs on Wall Street.

He now heads a highly respected PR firm based in the heart of downtown Las Vegas. In this role, Fierro provides litigation support for trials that draw regional and national media attention including serving as a consultant in the Michael Jackson wrongful death trial. As president of Fierro Communications, Inc., Fierro works with a team of dedicated writers and executives from his firm's headquarters in an elegantly refurbished 1940s home, one of the most historic structures in downtown Las Vegas.

ACKNOWLEDGMENTS

I want to thank my editor, Jeff Haney, for working long hours (including weekends) to corral all of the information that was so instrumental in writing this book.

Thank you to Molly Taylor, who provided valuable research and was a constant source of support for members of the Meyers family, particularly Kristal.

Thank you to David Purdy, cameraman, video editor and audio editor for the audio portion of book. David spent many hours with the family and worked with Kristal during the painful process of going through family albums just a few raw weeks after her mother's tragic death.

I'd like to thank Bob Meyers for his courageous decision to step forward to tell his wife's story. He gave freely of his time and unchecked emotions during the most gut-wrenching time of his life.

All of us on the team were consistently impressed by the tremendous manners and family values that were expressed by all the Meyers children: Kristal, Robert, Brandon and Matthew. They forced themselves to spend hours with us to let everyone know about their mother and who she really was.

I would also like to thank "Tammy's Girls" — Tara Estes, Nichole McLaughlin, Amanda Ahlstrom and McKenzie Webster — who were so generous with their time and memories of Tammy Meyers.

Made in the USA
Las Vegas, NV
10 March 2023